# The Brief Career of
# Eliza Poe

Miniature of Eliza Poe. *(Courtesy of The Free Library of Philadelphia.)*

# The Brief Career
# of Eliza Poe

Geddeth Smith

Rutherford ● Madison ● Teaneck
Fairleigh Dickinson University Press
London and Toronto: Associated University Presses

© 1988 by Associated University Presses, Inc.


Associated University Presses
440 Forsgate Drive
Cranbury, NJ 08512

Associated University Presses
25 Sicilian Avenue
London WC1A 2QH, England

Associated University Presses
2133 Royal Windsor Drive
Unit 1
Mississauga, Ontario
Canada L5J 1K5

**Library of Congress Cataloging-in-Publication Data**

Smith, Geddeth, 1934–
  The brief career of Eliza Poe.

  Bibliography: p.
  Includes index.
  1. Poe, Eliza, d. 1811.   2. Actors—United States—
Biography.   I. Title.
  PN2287.P56S65   1988        792'.028'0924 [B]        86-46406
  ISBN 0-8386-3317-X (alk. paper)

For
Francesca

# Contents

# Preface

WHEN ELIZA POE,[1] the actress—mother of Edgar Allan Poe—died in Richmond, Virginia, at the age of twenty-four, she had played with every important
theatrical company in the country. Her career had touched all of the finest
actors working in America during her lifetime: James Fennell, Thomas Cooper,
Ann Merry, Elizabeth Kemble Whitlock, Mrs. Oldmixon, John Bernard, and
Anne West, to name only a few; and just before her death she had appeared as
John Howard Payne's leading lady during his great successes in Boston.

From the point of view of an actor or actress working in today's theatre, Eliza
Poe's career is truly extraordinary. It ended when most actors today begin their
careers. And in its brief course she played nearly three hundred parts: among
them, Juliet, Ophelia, Cordelia, Lydia Languish, and Lady Teazle, as well as a
long line of heroines from the eighteenth-century sentimental comedies, comic
operas, farces, and poetic tragedies that were so popular during her lifetime,
plays that are little more than meaningless titles to us now, for they have long
ceased to be played, though they contain scenes of brilliant language and canny
theatricality, and they require actors of discipline and skill to bring off.

Eliza herself left no personal documents of her life, not even so much as a
signature, but the many available documents relating to her professional career
tell a vivid story of the apprenticeship served by this gifted young actress in the
superior repertory system that existed in the United States during the late 18th
and early 19th centuries, and in the light of these records Eliza emerges, not as
the obscure actress we often meet in biographies of her gifted son, but as a young
artist who had established a national reputation with her co-workers and the
public, and who, at the time of her tragic death, was ready to begin doing her
most important work.

# Acknowledgments

IT WAS MY GOOD FRIEND and fellow actor the late Tom Rutherfurd who introduced me to the story of Eliza Poe many years ago, and I am grateful to him for starting me on my fascinating journey into our country's theatrical past in search of the facts about Eliza's life and work. I am indebted also to all of Poe's biographers, all of whom write of Eliza, but it is Arthur Hobson Quinn who paid the most attention to Poe's parents, and his scholarly research on their careers has been an invaluable source and guide.

I have long been acquainted with the helpfulness of librarians, archivists, and local historians, but it was not until I began work on this biography that I learned how truly generous they can be with their time. The following have been of great help to me: Edwin C. Coleman, Rector of St. Michael's Episcopal Church in Charleston; Mildred K. Abraham and King Blackwell of the University of Virginia Library; Milton C. Russell, Ethel M. Slonaker, and Katherine M. Smith of the Virginia State Library; Lucile B. Portlock (an avid researcher and especially helpful to me in gathering important details of Eliza's appearances in Norfolk) and Peggy A. Haile of the Norfolk Public Library; Mary R. Ishaq and Jerry W. Cotten of the University of North Carolina Library; Bernard A. Bernier, Jr., Mary M. Ison, and Katherine F. Gould of the Library of Congress; Harold B. Gill, Jr., of the Colonial Williamsburg Foundation; Ronald E. Shibley of Historic Fredericksburg Foundation, Inc.; Jack Jackson of the Library of the Boston Athenaeum; Lyn Hart and Clayton E. Rhodes of the Enoch Pratt Free Library; Gloria C. Tucker of the Office of Clerk of Circuit Court County of Goochland, Virginia; Mark Stansbury, Deborah B. Kelley, John Martin, and Toni Boldrick of the Houghton Library of Harvard University; E. M. Sanchez-Saavedra and Betty Gray Gibson of the Valentine Museum of Richmond; Edward Wyatt of the *Petersburg Progress-Index*; Mrs. Hugh B. Cox of Historic Alexandria Foundation; John Melville Jennings and James Meehan of the Virginia Historical Society; Edith Rutherfurd Greathead of Richmond; Ward J. Childs of the Department of Records of the City of Philadelphia; James H. Bailey of the Department of Tourism of the City of Petersburg; Rose C. Ruffin of the Petersburg Chamber of Commerce; Anne S. Adams and Michael C. Walker of the Petersburg Public Library; Thomas L. Johnson of the South Caroliniana Library at the University of South Carolina; P. William Filby, Hester Rich, and

Richard J. Cox of the Maryland Historical Society; Gino Marone and Susan Bryl of the State Historical Society of Wisconsin; Patricia E. Sudnik of the University of Chicago Library; Jon Reynolds of the Georgetown University Library; James Bartlett of the William L. Clements Library at the University of Michigan in Ann Arbor; Susan Mainwaring of the Library Company of Philadelphia; William C. Pollard and Margaret Cook of the Earl Gregg Swem Library at the College of William and Mary in Virginia; Catherine E. Sadler of the Charleston Library Society; Edgar Allen Been III of the Portland (Maine) Public Library; Robinson Murray III of the New Hampshire Historical Society; Mrs. Leila B. Wood of Edenton, N.C.; Shirley E. Welch of the Maine Historical Society; John D. Cushing of the Massachusetts Historical Society; Helen Channing Pollock of New York City; Marie Ellis of the University Libraries of the University of Georgia; and Joyce Ann Tracy, Eleanor S. Adams, and Mary E. Brown of the American Antiquarian Society for their help in locating many helpful details in the superb collection of early American newspapers in that archive.

The miniature of Eliza is reproduced as a frontispiece by courtesy of the Rare Book Department of the Free Library of Philadelphia, and permission to quote from George Poe, Jr.'s letter to William Clemm, Jr., has been granted by the Enoch Pratt Free Library of Baltimore, Maryland.

I am grateful to both Emilie Jacobson of Curtis Brown, Ltd. and James McGlone of Seton Hall University for reading the manuscript and giving me constructive and helpful criticism and to Harry Keyishian of Fairleigh Dickinson University for bringing my manuscript to the attention of the Editorial Committee of Fairleigh Dickinson University Press.

# The Brief Career
## of Eliza Poe

1

# "The Market Lass"

BOSTON HARBOR must have been an impressive sight to nine-year-old Eliza Arnold. And as she peered over the rail of the ship *Outram*, her first look at the city of Boston itself must have been an even more impressive sight—and a welcome one too, because for her it marked the end of a winter crossing from England that had taken nearly two months. It was the third day of January in the year 1796, a quiet, cold, New England Sabbath.[1]

To a nine-year-old girl the end of the lonely journey across the Atlantic meant the end of close quarters, seasickness, heavy seas, and long days and nights of tedium. To most of her fellow travelers on the *Outram* the sight of the long-awaited port of Boston meant, above all, a safe arrival, for in the year 1796 a winter crossing was a dangerous undertaking. Men carefully made their wills before they embarked and set out to sea, where their only contact with the world outside their ship was when they "spoke" a passing vessel. Indeed, before Eliza and her fellow passengers had begun their passage, as the *Outram* lay at the mouth of the Thames at Gravesend, a heavy gale had damaged and dismantled many vessels and sunk a large West Indiaman, drowning every soul on board.[2] It had been an ominous prelude to a dangerous voyage.

But the long journey was now over, and as Eliza looked beyond the many masts and sails of the ships that crowded the harbor, and first caught sight of the tall spire of the North Church, the golden dome of the new State House, and the Memorial Tower on Beacon Hill, she could not but have been struck at how small a city Boston seemed compared to London, where she had been brought up.

Eliza was traveling with her mother, Mrs. Elizabeth Arnold, whom the Boston papers later described as a tall and graceful young woman in her middle twenties. She was an actress and singer from the Covent Garden Theatre in London, where Charles Powell, the current manager of Boston's new Federal Street Theatre, had recently hired her. Also traveling aboard the *Outram* with Mrs. Arnold and Eliza was a gentleman, Charles Tubbs, of whom very little is known except that he was in love with Mrs. Arnold, that he played the pianoforte (at that time a comparatively new instrument), and that he had a disagreeable temper. Completing the party was another actress, a Miss Green, also signed to play at the Federal Street Theatre.[3] Both of the actresses were important enough additions to the Boston company for the *Massachusetts Mercury* to announce their arrival and to welcome them as "valuable acquisitions" to the Boston theatre. Mrs. Arnold was soon to make her debut as first singing actress at the Federal Street Theatre.

Eliza's mother was one of many English actors and actresses to come to the United States during the 1790s. Important new theatres were being established, and there was a demand for trained actors. In England, where they did their recruiting, the American managers offered good salaries, and they succeeded in persuading many actors of considerable professional standing to make the trip across the Atlantic.[4]

Mrs. Arnold and Eliza were arriving at a time of great change and remarkable growth and activity in the American theatres. The American Company, already a venerable institution that for over forty years had dominated the theatres in all the major cities of the young country, was beginning at this time to lose its monopoly. Two of this company's former members were starting new theatres. Thomas Wignell, a well-known actor and at one time a co-manager of the American Company, had left that management and in partnership with the English composer and conductor Alexander Reinagle was beginning a new theatre in Philadelphia. And another actor, Joseph Harper, also a former member of the American Company, a quiet and courageous man with a strong will, was responsible for accomplishing an even more important feat in establishing the first theatres in the Puritan stronghold of New England, most importantly in Providence, Newport, and Boston.

Since it was in Boston that Mrs. Arnold was to make her debut, it can be assumed that like any English actress of her generation, she knew something of the struggle to establish the new theatre there, and like all the members of her profession, she would have rejoiced in the final victory over their arch enemy the Puritans.

The Puritan influence in Boston had not yielded without a struggle, however, and it had all come about recently. There had been no theatre in Boston prior to the Revolutionary War, for the Puritan fathers, in the name of virtue, religion, and thrift, had managed to put through the legislature in 1750 a law that made it an offense either to perform or to attend plays. This law had remained on the books for more than forty years when a new generation of Bostonians, displeased that Boston was the only important city in America that had no theatre, met at Faneuil Hall to organize a petition to have the law repealed. When Samuel Adams rose to speak in opposition to them, the assembly shouted him down. Sentiment was certainly running high when such a distinguished Bostonian was not even allowed a hearing. Despite the fact that three-fourths of the citizens in two town meetings voted for the repeal of the law in Boston, the legislature nonetheless still refused to grant their petition.

The citizens of Boston, however, were determined, and a group of them, in defiance of the legislature, built a temporary playhouse and to circumvent the law named it the New Exhibition Room. It was here that Joseph Harper, in partnership with Alexandre Placide, presented his first season during the summer and fall of 1792. He offered varied entertainments and, employing the old device that English actors had first used when the Licensing Act of 1737 had closed all the London theatres except the Theatre Royal, he billed such plays as John Home's *Douglas* and Richard B. Sheridan's *The School for Scandal* as "Moral Lectures."

Governor John Hancock was enraged. He condemned the "foreigners and aliens"—Harper was English and Placide French—who were openly flouting the law of 1750. As a result, a performance of *The School for Scandal* at the New Exhibition Room was stopped by the authorities and a warrant served on Harper. The patrons were outraged. Cries of "Go on!" "Go on!" rang through the house, and when the play did not go forward, some of the more militant members of the audience tore down the state coat of arms and trampled it underfoot. At length order was restored, and Harper was carried away under arrest. The next day in court he was released.

This incident brought results, however, for early the next year the old Puritan law was repealed, and construction of a new theatre, designed by the eminent architect Charles Bullfinch, was begun on Federal Street. It was completed in 1794, when it opened with great festivity and appropriate ceremony, including a prologue in verse composed especially for the opening by Boston's brilliant young poet, Robert Treat Paine, one of the theatre's staunch supporters.[5]

This had all been only two years before Eliza Arnold and her mother arrived. The Massachusetts seaport of Boston was a very English city, and in many ways it would have reminded any emigrant of London, though it was very much smaller, for its population was only some twenty-five thousand. The strollers that Eliza and her mother saw on the Boston Common were not unlike those they might see in St. James Park, and indeed everywhere they looked they saw reflected the very latest London fashions in dress and decor. Even the speech sounded English. But perhaps this was not surprising to them, because it had scarcely been a generation since the Revolutionary War, before which many Bostonians had considered themselves British.[6]

However comforting and familiar the atmosphere of Boston may have been to Eliza and her mother, there was startling and unsettling news awaiting them there. Hardly could they have lost their sea legs and settled in their lodgings than they learned that Charles Powell, who had been the manager of the Federal

Street Theatre since its opening and who had hired Mrs. Arnold to appear in what would be his third season there, had been abruptly fired by the trustees. Powell, angry but undaunted, immediately announced in the papers his intention of building a second theatre in Boston—it was to be called the Haymarket—and he began organizing a subscription for it.[7] But where did this leave Mrs. Arnold? She had made all of her arrangments with Powell, and her prospects of beginning a new life in America were dim if her contract with Powell was invalid or if she were to be forced to wait for the construction of his new theatre before she could even make her debut. The days following her arrival were anxious ones.

Fortunately, however, her services were in demand. The Federal Street Theatre needed a leading singing actress, and Joseph Harper, its newly appointed manager (the same Joseph Harper who had faced down the Puritan authorities and been arrested for his pains), took her into his company and set her debut for 12 February.

So it was only after a rather frightening beginning that Mrs. Arnold and Eliza could actually relax and begin to settle down in their furnished rooms in Mrs. Baylis's house on 14 State Street. They now had little over a month to get their bearings and prepare for the all-important night of the debut.

Certainly one of the first places they sought out while they were waiting for rehearsals to begin was the Federal Street Theatre, where the American Company was playing a guest engagement until the end of January. And if they saw one of this company's productions there, they would have been pleased with their impressions of the elegantly designed house in which Mrs. Arnold was soon to play.

It stood on the northwest corner of Franklin and Federal Streets and had been designed by Charles Bullfinch, later one of the architects for the Capitol in Washington, D.C. It was built of brick with some stone facings, iron posts, and pillars. There were an arcade for carriages and separate entrances to each part of the house as well as a restaurant and a ballroom. The interior decor reflected the delicate detail of the Adam style upon which Bullfinch was to build his reputation. The arched ceiling was supported by Corinthian columns, and the two rows of boxes were decorated with crimson silk and gilded balustrades. Azure, straw, and lilac were the colors on the walls and the fronts of the boxes. A capacity audience numbered slightly over a thousand. The thirty-one-foot proscenium opening was decorated on each side by two columns between which, in a design dating from Shakespeare's Globe Theatre, was a door opening onto the stage. Above each door projected an iron balcony, and above the proscenium itself were painted on a crimson drapery the arms of the United States and the Commonwealth of Massachusetts, the masks of comedy and tragedy, and a flowing ribbon with the motto "All the world's a stage."[8]

Harper began his season on 25 January.[9] From her first rehearsal Mrs. Arnold must have felt very much at home, because the bulk of the acting company was

English, some of whom, such as John Williamson and his wife Louisa Fontenelle Williamson, she had even known in London. The Williamsons were also making their American debuts that season, and Mrs. Arnold and Mrs. Williamson had both played at Covent Garden. The newly arrived actors found the Federal Street Theatre staffed with a highly professional company of performers and a well-organized production crew. Besides the actors, dancers, and musicians, the staff included a prompter, or stage manager, machinists, scene painters, wardrobe attendants, dressers, a lighting crew, fire attendants, doorkeepers, and a call boy.[10] An important and at that time unique position at the Federal Street Theatre was the master of ceremonies, whose responsibility it was "to preserve the order and decorum of the house . . . to take care, that the ladies and gentlemen are seated in their places, to which they are entitled by their tickets; to direct the disposition of the carriages in coming to and going from the theatre and generally to arrange the whole etiquette of the auditory and to prevent or suppress all kind of disorder and indecorum,"[11] including galleryites who thought nothing of pelting the stage with oranges and apple cores.

In order to attract audiences the staff of any eighteenth-century playhouse had to be capable of enormous productivity. Long runs were unheard of—there was no audience to support them—and in order to attract the public a theatre had to offer constant variety in its repertory. Actors were required to be versatile and to have repertoires of up to fifty or so stock parts, which they could play literally at the drop of a hat. In a season of fifteen to twenty weeks a theatre would regularly produce over a hundred different entertainments including plays, farces, burlettas, comic operas, pantomimes, and any number of interludes. It was usually open only three nights a week, but its standard nightly fare included at least two plays, often more.

This required highly disciplined actors, and strict professional standards were maintained by a system of fines. An actor could lose a week's salary if he refused to play a part assigned to him by the manager or if he appeared drunk on stage. He could lose a night's salary for not being ready in a part. Lesser fines were imposed for using the book on the final rehearsal, refusing to wear a costume provided by the management, and even for wearing a hat in the Green Room.[12]

Eliza's mother had been trained in the repertory system in England. She was very much at home in this professional world, and she was soon ready to make her debut. Few actors face any new audience without fear and uncertainty, and though she was playing a part she had often played before, Rosetta in Isaac Bickerstaffe's comic opera *Love in a Village*, Mrs. Arnold was facing an audience of complete strangers. Boston was not London, and her future in America depended on her winning the approval of a very different public. At the time the Boston public consisted of two distinct camps: the sedate and conservative Federalists who occupied the boxes (sending their servants to the theatre early in order to hold places for them, for no seats were reserved), and the unpredictable and sometimes rowdy Republicans of the gallery and pit, capable of hissing, foot-stamping, and abusive shouting, if they wished to show their disapproval. Such was the audience that Mrs. Arnold must please if she were to begin her career in America successfully.

Fortunately, her debut was a success. "The theatre never shook with such bursts of applause," effusively reported a writer for the *Massachusetts Mercury* in describing her debut. "Not a heart but was sensible of her merits; not a tongue but vibrated in her praise; not a hand but moved in approbation."[13]

Having won the favor of the Boston public, Mrs. Arnold continued to appear prominently at the Federal Street Theatre throughout the rest of the season, even sharing the leading role of Agnes in George Colman II's comic opera, *The Mountaineers,* with Mrs. Williamson, whose debut had also been a great success. She was also featured in *Traveller Returned,* a new play that created a great deal of interest in Boston, for it was written by an American, ostensibly a woman, but rumored to come from the pen of a man of the cloth, the Reverend John Murray.

Eliza, who during the season must surely have watched her mother's growing popularity with great enthusiasm, was herself soon to share in Mrs. Arnold's success. Every actor was entitled to at least one benefit a season, the proceeds of which, after the expenses of the house, went to the actor for whom the benefit was given. Despite the fact that they could be risky—for they could actually result in a loss of money to the actor if he failed to attract an audience large enough to cover the expenses—benefits were important nights. They not only had a personal significance in indicating what following the actor had won with the public, but they might also be profitable, in most instances adding to his income an amount equal to one-third his salary for the entire season.[14] They were always special occasions, and for her benefit on 15 April, a memorable night for Eliza, Mrs. Arnold played the leading roles in Miles Peter Andrew's romantic melodrama *Mysteries of the Castle* (a new play to Boston audiences) and in William Shield's short musical afterpiece *Rosina.*

Between these two plays she led her little daughter out on the stage in front of the candle footlights to sing a new song, "The Market Lass." Only three months after arriving in America, Eliza Arnold had begun her apprenticeship. She was nine years old.

## 2

# "A Miss of Only Nine Years Old"

IT WAS NOT LONG before Eliza again appeared before the Boston public. After the season at the Federal Street Theatre closed the middle of May, her mother sang at Bowen's Museum. Encouraged by her success in this concert, Mrs. Arnold presented another one a week later in the ballroom of the theatre, and it was then that Eliza made her second public appearance. She sang "The Market Lass" and added a new song to her repertoire, "Henry's Cottage Maid."

A number of the theatre's orchestra members took part in this concert, including the composer and conductor, who, like so many of the early professional musicians in America, were French, probably two of the many court musicians who had fled to America from France during the French Revolution. Besides featuring Eliza on the program, Mrs. Arnold herself introduced several new songs. One of them, "The Cottage Gate," had words by the playwright Richard B. Sheridan and music by Joseph Hayden, and she sang it from manuscript. After the concert, music was provided for a ball.[1]

Now that Eliza had made her debut as a singer, her mother made an important and far-reaching decision for the nine-year-old girl. She decided to bring her out as an actress. It was a logical and even an economic decision on Mrs. Arnold's part, and Eliza, like any child, probably accepted it casually. She had been born into the theatre, and it was the only life she would ever know.

If Eliza was to become an actress, it was necessary for her to play a line of demanding parts somewhere so that she could begin gaining the experience and building the repertoire that would make her useful in a professional company. It would have been impossible for her to do this had Mrs. Arnold sought work in Hartford, Providence, or Newport, where many of the Boston actors had gone to play short summer engagements, so she began making other plans.

Two years earlier Snelling Powell, an actor with whom she had played at the Federal Street Theatre, had been responsible for presenting the first theatrical season in the small New England seaport of Portland, Maine.[2] With his wife and a small company he had enjoyed enthusiastic audiences. There had been no season in Portland since then, but with the new theatres in full swing in Boston, Providence, and Newport, it seemed reasonable to Mrs. Arnold that Portland would again welcome actors. Portsmouth, New Hampshire, another seaport, was on the way to Portland, and it too was a good prospect. With herself, Eliza, and a small company she could present a short season in these towns, just as Snelling Powell had done.

In a Puritan community it would be necessary to begin carefully—with a concert. That would be respectable enough. Then, once she had found an audience and made some personal contacts with the local citizens, it would be possible with a few more actors, and even some local amateurs if necessary, to present a number of short plays. The venture could even be profitable, for in themselves plays were a novelty in New England, particularly in the smaller towns. Eliza would have the opportunity she needed to begin her training and would even be an asset, for child performers always have a special appeal. So in the early summer, she and Eliza set out for New England. Traveling with them was Charles Tubbs.

Indeed, Charles Tubbs himself was a strong reason why Mrs. Arnold planned to play in Portsmouth and Portland. Whether he was engaged to marry her before they left Boston for New England or even earlier when he first arrived in the United States with her and Eliza on the *Outram*, it is unknown. Tubbs, however, wanted to become an actor, and he had no experience. He played the pianoforte and could accompany both Mrs. Arnold and Eliza in concerts, but as an actor he could be even more active. It was a time when managers often found it practical to hire married couples and sometimes even whole families, and if he, Eliza, and Mrs. Arnold planned to work together, it was necessary that Tubbs also, like Eliza, begin building a repertoire and gaining some experience as an actor.


It took courage for the small party of three to set out on their trip. They had hardly been six months in America, and though they did not face the terrible struggles of actors attempting to practice their trade in America before the Revolutionary War, it was still Puritan New England where they sought the audience that would provide them their livelihood. They were also British, toward whom many of the patriotic citizens of the smaller New England towns were still very hostile.[3]

There were two ways to travel from Boston to Portsmouth in the summer of 1796, by sea in a packet or by land in a stage wagon, and the length of the trip either way depended on the weather. Under good conditions it took the stage, drawn by a team of four horses, a full day to travel the fifty or so miles. If Eliza made the trip with her mother and Charles Tubbs by land, they traveled in a "Flying Machine" (so named when this latest design of stage wagon or stage coach, as it was later known, made the New York-Philadelphia run in the record time of a day and a half). The "Flying Machine" was little more than an open wagon covered with a flat top and fitted with curtains on the sides. The newer models featured benches with backs (the older models had had no backs on the benches) and even leather springs to make the ride more comfortable. Any trip was still a bumpy and exhausting ordeal, and the roads could be treacherous, often making it necessary for the passengers to make part of their journey on foot to ease the load of the wagon over the deep ruts in the road, or "to lean out of the carriage, first on one side, then on the other, to prevent it from oversetting."[4]

Whether they traveled by packet or stage wagon, Eliza, her mother, and Charles Tubbs were in Portsmouth by mid-July and they began planning for their debut there. One of their first discoveries in Portsmouth was that they were not the only performers who had the idea of touring New England that summer, for when they arrived, they found that Don Pedro Cloris the rope dancer, Merryman the Clown, and Mr. Salenka and "The Knowing Dog" were all appearing regularly at the town's Assembly Room.[5]

Mrs. Arnold promptly rented the Assembly Room for Wednesday, 3 August, and took advertisements in both of the triweekly Portsmouth papers. In the advertisements she billed herself as a singer from Boston and announced that she would present a concert featuring herself and Eliza as singers accompanied by Tubbs on the pianoforte. Eliza was to sing "The Market Lass" and "Henry's Cottage Maid." As in their last concert in Boston, music was to be provided for "those ladies and gentlemen who choose to have a ball after the concert." Admission was $1.00 per couple.

The concert was a success, and Mrs. Arnold presented a second one two weeks later in the Assembly Room. Again she and Eliza both sang, Tubbs accompanied them and also played a solo, and once more the concert was followed by a ball.

By this time they had been in Portsmouth over a month and had succeeded in placing themselves before the public. The concerts and balls had given them the opportunity of meeting many of the townspeople, of making some friends, and they had also had ample time to feel out any Puritan influence. By late August Mrs. Arnold was ready to make definite plans for the production of their first plays. She set the opening for Monday, 5 September, at the Assembly Room, announced it in both papers, and began rehearsals.

The plays for the opening night were those popular standbys of the late eighteenth century, John Home's verse tragedy *Douglas* and, as the afterpiece, Isaac Bickerstaffe's farce *The Spoiled Child.* A good choice for the opening play, *Douglas* was written in blank verse with long speeches, plenty of rhetoric, and what its contemporary audiences would have called "affecting sentiment," including that favorite and stock device of the eighteenth century, a tearful family reunion, in this case a mother and son. *Douglas* was, moreover, a tragedy with good moral content, so that the Puritans could not call it frivolous. It had even been written by a Scottish minister (the Portsmouth audience need not know that its author, John Home, was finally compelled to resign his ministry on his play's account). Most important of all, from the practical point of view, the play had a small cast. *The Spoiled Child* also had a small cast. It was a knockabout farce centered around the pranks of a wild and uncontrollable boy, aptly named Little Pickle and usually played by a grown actress since the role included good songs, several disguises, and was an excellent vehicle for a clever comedienne.

Heading the small company at the Assembly Room were Mrs. Arnold, Eliza, and Charles Tubbs, and joining them to play Little Pickle was their friend and fellow passenger on the *Outram*, Miss Green. There were also a number of local amateurs.

From early September to early November, a period of ten weeks, this small company, strengthened later in its season by the addition of two more professional actors, produced thirteen widely different plays ranging from poetic tragedy to farce. This was an enormous output.

The conditions under which they worked were primitive. The Assembly Room at Portsmouth was a far cry from the gilded balustrades of the Federal Street Theatre; but it is important to remember that the theatre in which Eliza grew up was, in the real sense, an actors' theatre. "I was performer, machinist, painter, designer, music compiler, the bill maker, and treasurer,"[6] wrote her contemporary John Durang in his *Memoir*. And in the off season, when actors were away from whatever engagements they might have in the theatres of the larger towns, they set up performances exactly as Eliza's mother had, sometimes even building their own stages. It was taken for granted, an important part of their income and training. Even the great actress Sarah Siddons, who with her brother John Phillip Kemble stood undisputedly at the head of her profession in England, had served this same kind of apprenticeship under her father, Roger Kemble; and in her prime at the height of her career in London, an audience member could still remember his impression of the great actress "as a child . . . a solitary figure in the draughty wings of the rustic theatre, banging a pair of snuffers against a candlestick to produce the monotonous sound of a windmill off the stage."[7] Eliza was beginning her apprenticeship in this same tradition.

Eliza played every night that the improvised theatre in the Assembly Room was open, and some of her assignments were important ones. She played the leading roles in two of the afterpieces: Biddy Belair in Garrick's farce *Miss in Her Teens* and Polly, the heroine in George Colman I's farce *Polly Honeycombe*. There were also the dark-eyed gipsy Zorayda in *The Mountaineers*, the rustic farm girl Phoebe in William Shield's *Rosina*, the maid Lucy in *The Devil to Pay*, and Lavinia in Nicholas Rowe's verse tragedy *The Fair Penitent*. Her most difficult assignment was Constance Neville in the small company's production of *She Stoops to Conquer*. In all she played twelve different parts. It was her first appearance as an actress, and an extraordinary beginning for a nine-year-old girl, to say the least.

The season at the Assembly Room succeeded far beyond Mrs. Arnold's expectations. She found an enthusiastic public, and in the last weeks of her company's engagement she began seeking local support to build a theatre in Portsmouth.[8]

Her plan was to begin building immediately so that the theatre could open the following May and play through the summer. She announced her proposals in *The Oracle of the Day*, promising to hire good performers and to appear herself at least twice a week during the season. The theatre, which was to contain a pit, gallery, and boxes, would cost approximately $1,500 to build and was to be financed by thirty shares of $50 each, payable by installments as the work required. The building would be under the control of the subscribers. As manager, Mrs. Arnold would lease it for five years at an agreed-upon rent. The money was to be raised by subscription, and Mrs. Arnold had the subscription paper with her during the last performances at the Assembly Room.

If these plans materialized, she, Eliza, and Tubbs would be assured of an engagement in the summer and still be able to play in the larger cities during the fall and winter. It would give them year-round employment.

Meantime, they set off for Portland, Maine.

Sometime before they arrived in Portland or shortly after their arrival there, Charles Tubbs married Eliza's mother,[9] and as head of the family he took charge of both Eliza's and her mother's careers. This was to prove unfortunate.

With hardly a season under his belt as an actor, Tubbs became a manager, and though they began in Portland with a concert as they had in Portsmouth, there was no careful wooing of the public as his wife had so skillfully done in Portsmouth. Immediately Tubbs announced that he would set up a theatre and perform "some of the most admired plays and farces."[10]

In the same paper in which his advertisement for the opening night performance appeared, Tubbs, Eliza, and Mrs. Tubbs (as she now billed herself) read this editorial comment: "A theatre will be opened in this town tomorrow evening. While we cultivate the strictest morality, we wish not to abridge our fellow citizens of rational amusements. Happily our Constitution and laws secure to us the enjoyment of freedom. May we never abuse it!"[11] This was the first hint of opposition they had met on their trip into New England, and this spectre of the old Puritan prejudice must have sent a chill down their spines.

There was nothing to do but go on, however, and they began rehearsals. Again the theatre was the town's Assembly Room. Located on the second floor of the Portland Assembly Hall on India Street, it held an audience of about seventy to a hundred. The room itself measured approximately thirty-five by twenty-seven feet and was heated by two six-foot fireplaces at either end, a necessary protection against the bitter cold New England winter. Their stage was little more than a small platform, measuring fifteen by seven feet, a cramped and inadequate area for any play.

For the opening night Tubbs chose to play Isaac Bickerstaffe's comic opera *The Padlock* followed by *Miss in Her Teens* featuring Eliza in the leading role of Biddy Belair.

If the cool reception Tubbs's announcement had already had in the Portland paper made him and his family circle uneasy, their hopes were even more dampered by the late arrival of the other actors. Charles Clapham and Mr. Partridge, both professional actors who had joined their company toward the end of the Portsmouth season and whom Tubbs had also engaged for the Portland season, arrived in town very late for rehearsals. This was unfortunate, for Tubbs had chosen to open with *The Padlock,* a play they had not played together in Portsmouth.

There was still another portent. As the actors watched the first night audience file into the little Assembly Room, they saw that it was composed of only men, an indication, the actors would have recognized immediately, that the community was taking no chances as to the respectability of the performance. It was a stuffy and uncomfortable situation.

Predictably, the audience was unenthusiastic about the performance, and one of the men reported his impressions of the opening night in an unsigned letter to the *Eastern Herald and Gazette of Maine.* He objected to the cutting of the plays (made necessary by the small company), and also to certain expressions of obscenity and profanity. The ladies of Portland should not attend, it was his opinion, until they could be sure of not being offended. Fortunately, his letter was not all unfavorable. He liked Mrs. Tubbs and Clapham and was delighted with Eliza's performance: "Miss Arnold, in Miss Biddy, exceeded all praise. Although a Miss of only nine years old, her powers as an actress would do credit to any of her sex of maturer age."[12]

The opening was not a complete disaster, however. The letter in the paper had at least created some interest with the public, and Eliza had attracted attention.

The company next performed Arthur Murphy's comedy *The Citizen* and the farce *Trick upon Trick,* and the theatrical correspondant (as his contemporaries would have called him), undoubtedly encouraged by seeing his opinions in print, again wrote to the Portland paper. This time he praised the entire company, including the manager Tubbs, for the improvement; and he even recommended that the ladies of the town attend the plays. Again he had warm praise for Eliza, who played a new role, Solomon Smack, in the farce.[13]

With more favorable publicity the actors were now on a better footing, and in the three and a half weeks before Christmas they played eight nights, producing fifteen plays and one pantomime. Six of these productions were new; they had not done them in Portsmouth. This was again an enormous amount of work, but not at all unusual for actors of that day.

Eliza was a valuable asset to the small company. Not only did she play important roles, but she soon became a favorite with the audiences and consistently won praise in the letters published in the papers. Tubbs gave her a benefit, the first of her career, the week before Christmas. She played Phoebe in *Rosina,* a part she had played in Portsmouth, and her mother was in the title role. In the afterpiece, *The Spoiled Child,* Eliza played Little Pickle. This was her first time to play Little Pickle, a role that was to become an important part of her repertoire, and the evening was a great success.

> Mrs. Tubbs always does well. Her vocal powers we believe are equal to any of her sex who have appeared in this country. But the powers of her daughter, Miss Arnold, astonish us. Add to these her youth, her beauty, her innocence, and a character is composed which has not, and perhaps will not again ever be found on any Theatre.—Lovely child! thy youth we know will not long continue; thy beauty soon must fade; but thy innocence! may it continue with and support thee in every character while on the theatre of this world.[14]

Tubbs did not fare so well. It was conceded that as a manager he possessed the ability and the desire to please, and that some of his productions were successful, particularly the spirited performance of the pantomime *Harlequin Skeleton* and Robert Dodsley's *The King and the Miller of Mansfield,* both of which had created genuine enthusiasm; but his lack of experience had accounted for too many "imperfections in the choice or cast of the plays."[15] Moreover, he was told with good old-fashioned Yankee candor that though he performed well on the piano, he simply could not sing and should not even attempt it. When he cast two young gentlemen from Portsmouth in important parts, it drew an outburst in the papers. They had never before appeared in public! "Every one of the audience was compelled to suppress indignation, and seemed literally to sweat for relief. The exhibition and the sweat continued for about an hour and a half! . . . the Manager ought to have known better. Nay, Charity herself will say—either he did know better, and should in future do better, or that he should shut up the house and go home."[16]

By the end of December the New England winter had set in, and on the cold nights audiences were small. Several performances were even postponed on account of weather; but instead of closing the week before Christmas, as he had originally planned, Tubbs decided to extend his season two weeks beyond the holidays and finally closed on 17 January.

For Eliza it had been an especially successful engagement. She had proved herself to be a very talented and precocious girl and an attractive and promising performer. She had also borne up under the pressure of a stiff workload. There was no question that she could become a fine actress. All she needed was experience and guidance in developing her repertoire. Her success in Portland had been modest, her mother realized, by the strictest professional standards, but nonetheless it was a strong beginning. And as an appropriate end to a strong beginning, Eliza stepped out on the tiny platform stage in the Assembly Hall on the company's closing night and spoke an original farewell epilogue written especially for her by an anonymous Portland admirer.

> Ladies and gentlemen, I come with heart
> Oppress'd with grief that we so soon must part—
> Must part! my bosom swells! excuse, I pray
> The flowing tears! I'll wipe them thus away
>               (*Wiping her eyes*)
> Now I am mistress of myself again
>               (*Cheerfully*)
> And female fortitude shall conquer pain
> But, tho' I thus suppress the starting tear,
> Believe me, gratitude shall flourish here
>               (*Laying her hand on her bosom*)
> Accept my warmest thanks for favors shown;
> I claim no merit—candor is your own.
> But tho' to merit I can lay no claim
> To please has been my never ceasing aim;
> And to effect this end, to me you find
> What various characters have been assigned,
> A miss just in her teens, a rigid *nurse*,
> A boy to please old maids, O lud, that's worse;
> Sometimes I have appeared a ghost, tis true,
> But yet I'm flesh and blood—as well as you;
> A sailor too—"O pity, pity" Jack—
> Sun in a cloud and taken all aback
> A lover I have been—but how perplexing!
> And to our sex the thing is always vexing!
> But, ladies, pardon me 'twas by direction
> And nothing—nothing—nothing but a fiction
> And yet we talk of *love* and Cupid's darts;
> And is it hard that *ladies* should have *hearts?*
> I'm sure that I have one, I feel it here,
>               (*Laying her hand on her bosom*)
> Lest I offend, it palpitates with fear.
> But what have I to fear? in what offended?
> If aught I've done amiss, I'll strive to mend it:
> Meantime a Portland audience appears,
> And, smiling, pleads the cause of tender years.
> 'Twas here to be expected: Fame spoke true
> And every word is verified in you;
> For if we search the continent around,
> More genuine candor no where can be found.
> Tho' now I, like a bird of passage fly,
> To breathe a while beneath a milder sky,
> Where Phoebus' rays with stronger ardor burn,

With a still stronger ardor shall I seek return.
Then may I hope at a maturer age,
Indulg'd by you, to tread the Portland stage
(*The bell rings*)
But hark! to me how pensive sounds that bell!
Kind patrons! may I call you such! *Farewell!*[17]

The week following their closing in Portland, Tubbs, Eliza, and her mother were back in Portsmouth, where they were joined by Joseph Harper and his wife.[18] Harper and Tubbs agreed to become co-managers and to reopen the Assembly Room for a short engagement. Afterward they planned to play in Providence and Newport, where Harper managed two new theatres.

Joseph Harper would have been very keenly interested in Mrs. Tubbs's plan for establishing a theatre in Portsmouth, for he, more than anyone, had been responsible for breaking down the Puritan prejudices against the theatre in New England. He had been actively involved in the struggle to start the theatre in Boston, and as a result of his arrest in that struggle was a distinguished and well-known public figure. Mrs. Tubbs had worked under his management at the Federal Street Theatre, and if she did enlist his help in her plans for the Portsmouth theatre, he would be able to give her excellent advice, for he was a highly experienced and successful manager. Should they succeed in building the theatre in Portsmouth, it would be easy to do the same in Portland; and then with Harper's theatres in Providence and Newport, they would have a New England circuit.

The company with which Tubbs and Harper opened in the Portsmouth Assembly Room on 1 February was stronger than the one Mrs. Tubbs had presented there the preceding fall. The Harpers, Mrs. Tubbs, and Clapham were all professionals; and though Charles Tubbs, Eliza, and Tubbs's Portland recruits, King and Peters (both of whom had also come on to Portsmouth), were just beginning their careers, they all had some experience. Partridge was no longer with them, but this time it could at least be said that there were, technically, no amateurs.

Eliza played every night that Harper and Tubbs opened their theatre in the Assembly Room. Twice she played Little Pickle, giving her Portsmouth public the first opportunity to see her in the role, and on the company's final night she played a new role, Prince Edward in an interlude from George Colman II's *Margaret of Anjou.* The interlude was a dramatic scene lifted from the play, and Eliza was featured in it with the Harpers.

Shortly after the closing night, the company left for Rhode Island. Unfortunately, however, they had not succeeded in finding strong local backing, and Mrs. Tubbs' plans for the new Portsmouth theatre were still very uncertain.

After the makeshift stages they had played on in the Assembly Rooms of Portsmouth and Portland, the actors would have all welcomed the opportunity to play in real theatres again, and both theatres that Harper managed in Rhode Island were not only well designed but also new.

The theatre in Newport occupied the top two floors of the brick market house. It had been opened three years earlier, in 1793, by Harper and Alexandre Placide. A small house with one gallery, it seated about three hundred.[19]

The Providence Theatre was larger and built of wood. It was only two years old, and in order for it to open on time the Providence carpenters had formed a bee and stopped all other work until the theatre was completed. Such was the support Harper had from his public.[20] Its design was based on the famous old John Street Theatre in New York (one of the first homes of the American Company), so that it had a pit, boxes, and gallery, each with its outside entrance. The middle entrance, to the boxes, was covered with a wooden canopy. Like many theatres of the period, the dressing rooms were under the stage on the sides and separated by the trap room in the center. The proscenium opening was ample, sixteen feet high and twenty-six feet wide, and above the traditional green curtain and the proscenium arch, its motto told something of the story of Harper's struggle with the Puritans: "Pleasure the means—the end virtue."[21]

Harper and Tubbs first planned to play in Newport, where the Kennas joined their company. Mr. and Mrs. Kenna were both well known actors, at one time managing their own theatre, the Northern Liberties, outside Philadelphia. Mrs. Kenna had the distinction of having played with Harper in the first performances of Royall Tyler's play *The Contrast* (one of the American Company's great successes and the first highly successful play to be written by an American).

The Harper-Tubbs company opened the Newport Theatre on 28 March.[22] They presented a short season of five nights over a period of three weeks with substantially the same repertory that their company had played in Portland. Eliza played both Solomon Smack and Little Pickle, but there were no new parts for her to learn, and with the company strengthened by the addition of the Kennas there were fewer assignments for her than she had had in the busy weeks in Portland and Portsmouth. Both her mother and Tubbs were cast in important roles, and Mrs. Tubbs was given a benefit.

The actors moved to the Providence Theatre on 16 April, and for the opening four days later Eliza, her mother, and Charles Tubbs all announced their Providence debuts: Tubbs as Papillon in Samuel Foote's *The Lyar* and Eliza and her mother as the Girl and Josephine in Thomas Morton's play *Children in the Wood.*[23]

During their second week in Providence, Tubbs, in the first show of temper to mark his short career as an actor and manager, had a dispute with Harper, and he left the company taking his wife and Eliza with him. Announcing in the paper that he had "relinquished all connection with Mr. Harper,"[24] Tubbs took the Providence Theatre for one night and presented a concert for the benefit of

Mrs. Tubbs featuring songs and duets by Eliza and her mother with himself on the pianoforte.

On their own again, Mr. and Mrs. Tubbs and Eliza returned to Newport, where they presented another concert with readings at Mrs. Penrose's Hall in Church Street, advertising their program in the *Newport Mercury* as "Oddities or a Certain Cure for the Spleen." They had competition in attracting an audience, however, for Harper had also returned to Newport, and on the same night of their concert he was playing with his company at the Newport Theatre.[25]

Meantime, Eliza had had a birthday. She was now billed as "a young lady 10 years of age."[26]

# The John Street Theatre

IT HAD NOW BEEN a year since Eliza's debut, and a very active and full year it had been. During the New England tour she had learned and played a dozen or more roles, some of them important and demanding ones, and most of them good, standard vehicles for a child actress. Under her mother's guidance she had developed a small and selective repertoire that would make her useful to a theatrical manager. What she now needed was the experience of working with seasoned actors in a highly professional company, and in August 1797 she had this opportunity when along with her mother and stepfather she joined John Sollee's company in Hartford, Connecticut.

There is no record of exactly when Eliza traveled from Newport to Hartford with her mother and Tubbs, but she spent a good part of the summer with them there, because when Sollee hired them all in August, he gave them an advance to pay a large bill for board.[1] If they had gone to Hartford directly from Newport, hoping to find work immediately, they were disappointed and stranded, for there was no work for them at the Hartford Theatre until late in the summer when Sollee hired them. On the other hand, if they had known of Sollee's company and his plans to play in Hartford, they may have arranged to meet him there. In either case, they were in Hartford and probably without work for most of the summer.

John Sollee, "a very genteel, acute Frenchman,"[2] as the playwright William Dunlap described him, was the manager of the City Theatre in Charleston, South Carolina. He was in Hartford to present his company in a short engagement, after which he planned to play both New York and Philadelphia before taking his company to Charleston for the fall. Sollee had formed his present company in Boston that summer, hiring many of his actors there; he had also just arranged to begin an exchange between the theatres of Boston and Charleston.[3]

This Boston-Charleston exchange had come about as a result of the opening of the Haymarket Theatre in Boston during the season that Eliza was on the New England tour. True to his word, Charles Powell had opened a second theatre in Boston and called it the Haymarket. It had given the Federal Street Theatre stiff competition, and Boston had had a very difficult time supporting both theatres simultaneously. Losses at the Federal Street Theatre were disastrous, and at the end of the season, John Sollee and John Hodgkinson, one of the managers of the American Company, took both Boston theatres. Their plan was to organize the actors playing at the Haymarket and Federal Street Theatres in Boston and the City Theatre in Charleston into two companies that would play alternate seasons in both cities. In this way, they reasoned, the two theatres in Boston would no longer play in competition.

From Sollee's point of view this was a particularly attractive arrangement, for it meant that his own company in Charleston would be considerably strengthened, and he would be able to offer his Charleston public an excellent company and an impressive repertory.

It was for the company first to play in Charleston and then to play the following year in Boston that Sollee hired Eliza, her mother, and Charles Tubbs.

For his short season at the Hartford Theatre, Sollee cast Eliza as Maria in *The Spoiled Child*.[4] Maria, Little Pickle's sister, is a secondary part, and it was one of the first roles Eliza had played in Portsmouth. In the part of Little Pickle was Louisa Fontenelle Williamson.

Though Eliza had herself enjoyed some success as Little Pickle and there was little excitement for her in being cast in the smaller, less pivotal role, it was nonetheless very important for her to work in the play with Mrs. Williamson, for Little Pickle was one of Mrs. Williamson's greatest successes, and she was a brilliant actress. Robert Treat Paine described her American debut, which had occurred in Boston the same season as Eliza's mother's, as "the most astonishing and brilliant display of theatrical genius ever exhibited in America."[5] The English poet Robert Merry spoke of her "animal spirits" as being like "brandy above proof!"[6] and Robert Burns, also a great admirer of Mrs. Williamson, wrote several poems for her, one of them an epilogue, which she was fond of reciting on her benefit nights.[7]

For the apprentice Eliza playing with such a distinguished actress was excellent training. However frustrating it was for her to watch Mrs. Williamson's performance as Little Pickle (it was bound to be far more polished than her own attempt at the part), her association with this accomplished actress would have made a deep and lasting impression on the precocious girl. Learning the difficult art of acting depends to a great extent on absorbing a living tradition, and it is by playing with skillful and mature actors that an apprentice does this. In the repertory system that prevailed during her lifetime, Eliza was to receive all of her training in this way.

After closing in Hartford, John Sollee, according to plan, moved his company to New York City, which in 1798 covered only the tip of Manhattan Island and was dwarfed by the magnificent bay and surrounding countryside. Eliza found it a very different place from any of the New England towns she had visited. English was not the only language she heard on the streets, and everywhere she could still see strong traces of the Dutch and old New Amsterdam. The streets had Dutch names, and there were houses of yellow Holland brick with elaborately hand-wrought iron dates on their walls marking the year of their construction. Some of them dated from the seventeenth century. These old Dutch buildings stood alongside newer and elegant Georgian and Federal rowhouses. From Battery Park, Eliza could see porpoises playing in the Hudson River and only a few blocks north of Park Row, where the new Park Theatre was under construction, she could walk beyond the Collect, a large fresh water pond fed by underground springs, into the country. Everything was within walking distance: Trinity Church, St. Paul's Church, and Federal Hall, a striking landmark but no longer the seat of the federal government, for in 1790 Philadelphia had replaced New York as the nation's capitol. There were also Fraunces Tavern, the Tontine Coffee House that housed the growing New York Stock Exchange, and the John Street Theatre, where Eliza would soon play.

The John Street Theatre, a large wooden structure of a rough, functional design, was painted the usual dull red of the old colonial theatres (for it had been built before the Revolutionary War). It was on the north side of John Street about half a dozen doors from Broadway, set back about sixty feet from the street with a long covered passageway at the entrance. There were a pit, gallery, and a double tier of boxes. The stage was unusually large, and though the dressing rooms and greenroom were originally located underneath the stage, by the time Eliza played there, they had been moved to an added wing of the building. It had first opened in 1767, and for a generation of actors and audiences had served as the New York home of the American Company, which at the time Eliza arrived in New York was away from New York on tour and would not return until the late fall to open its new theatre on Park Row. It was in this company's absence that Sollee had arranged to play at the John Street Theatre.[8]

For the opening night on Friday, 18 August, Eliza was again cast in the afterpiece, as she had been in Hartford, as Maria in *The Spoiled Child*. Sollee gave her special billing, announcing that it was her first appearance in New York and that as Maria she would also have a song.

This was Eliza's first engagement in an up-to-strength, highly professional company, for the actors that Sollee had assembled formed one of the three most important troupes then working in America (the other two being the American Company based in New York and Thomas Wignell's company in Philadelphia). Her assignments would be minor ones, and to a child actress full of energy and ready to step forward and be noticed, this was bound to be frustrating; nonetheless, appearing as a member of a first-rate company was important, and the exposure she would have to the actors with whom she worked would prove invaluable to her. Though she was no longer in a child's world, Eliza would have learned as a child learns, by listening, by observing, by absorbing, by imitation.

Cast in small and thankless parts, an apprentice actress must often begin in this way. She is fortunate if at the beginning of her career she can see the best actors' work—and Eliza was fortunate. Not long after the opening in New York, in an altogether unexpected turn of events, she had the opportunity to see an extraordinary group of actors perform.

Word of a yellow-fever epidemic in Philadelphia reached New York. The smallest rumor of this dreaded disease, which plagued the country during the 1790s, was enough to turn a bustling city into a deserted ghost town, for those people who did not evacuate stayed behind tightly closed doors to avoid contagion.

News of the fever in Philadelphia put an end to Sollee's plans for his company to play there. It was too early for him to go on south to Charleston, where the heat made it impractical to open until the late fall, so rather than disband his company and risk losing his actors, he arranged to extend his stand at the John Street Theatre into the early weeks of the fall. Not long after his decision to stay in New York, he discovered to his great surprise that he had a formidable competitor. Thomas Wignell's company from Philadelphia had opened several blocks away at the Greenwich Street Theatre.

The presence of both Sollee's and Wignell's companies in Manhattan gave New Yorkers a brilliant late-summer season during which at least one of the two theatres was open every night—an unheard-of state of affairs in those days, when theatres were accustomed to play only three nights a week. It also meant that a group of brilliant actors were playing at the same time in New York, most of whom a visiting Londoner would have recognized as having appeared prominently at Covent Garden or Drury Lane.[9]

At the John Street Theatre, Eliza had the opportunity of watching carefully the work of two superb actresses in the same company in which she herself was appearing. She was playing in support of Mrs. Williamson in *The Spoiled Child* and had already worked closely with this noted comedienne. Then, in the third week of her stand at the John Street Theatre, Eliza sang on the same bill with Elizabeth Kemble Whitlock, who with her husband, Charles Whitlock, joined Sollee's company. Mrs. Whitlock was the sister of the great Sarah Siddons and a member of the distinguished Kemble family of actors. She was a versatile and powerful actress.

On her night off Eliza could walk with her mother the few blocks to Greenwich Street where Wignell's company was playing and here see in the same company some of the most eminent actors of her generation: Ann Merry, Mrs. Oldmixon, James Fennell, Thomas Cooper, William Warren, John Bernard. She did not know it then, but it would not be long before she would be working with them all.

Sollee had an excellent company, but in facing such a strong competitor as he had on Greenwich Street, there were serious disadvantges in his appealing to the public. Though he had both Mrs. Whitlock and Mrs. Williamson as his leading actresses, he lacked a leading actor who could compare with either James Fennell or Thomas Cooper, both of whom were appearing at the Greenwich Street Theatre. Fennell, a tall and imposing figure and a master of spoken English, was the leading tragedian in America, and Cooper, though still very young and erratic, was a handsome and dynamic performer, just beginning to come into his own. Sollee's lack of a leading actor of stature seriously limited his choice of plays, and, unfortunately, along with his incomplete knowledge of English, also accounted for his presenting a much weaker repertory than his competitor. His company was also new. Many of them had not played together very long, and important members, notably the Placides, who could have added distinction and variety to his repertory, were waiting to join him in Charleston. But Sollee did have one trump card.

Before leaving Boston he had gotten the rights to a new play, *The Battle of Bunker Hill and the Death of General Warren,* written by John Daly Burk, an Irish journalist and political refugee. The premiere of Burk's play, which had taken place in Boston the preceding season, had been a great success, earning its author the then enormous sum of $2,000. It had not yet been performed outside Boston, and early in his run at the John Street Theatre, Sollee began rehearsals for its New York premiere.[10]

Eliza was cast in a walk-on part, as one of the young women dressed in white, holding flowers and accompanying the solemn procession just before the end of the play. With a demure countenance she held one hand on the bier of General Warren, the Revolutionary War hero, while her mother, as Sollee's first singing actress, sang the elegy with which the play ended. Tubbs, the erstwhile manager and leading actor of the New England tour, was probably, like Eliza, in a walk-on role as one of the soldiers in the American army, which moved slowly in the procession to the sound of solemn music.

Burk's play was primarily a spectacle that appealed strongly to the patriotism of a young country, and during Eliza's lifetime, it was to become a standard item in almost every theatre's repertory. Ten-year-old Eliza had the distinction of being in its second production. As in any play of the period a great deal of the spectacle for the audience was in the carefully and meticulously painted canvas drops. In Sollee's production they were painted by John Audin, a very well-known scenic artist, and they were advertised in detail as a special and important feature of the evening's entertainment. It was the day of heroic historical painting, and Audin depicted the burning of Charlestown and the engagement on Bunker Hill. These were stirring scenes to Revolutionary War veterans and the New York citizens who could still remember the British occupation of New York during the Revolutionary War, and it brought in Sollee's best business. The battle scenes, in which Tubbs would also have appeared, were elaborately staged. Burk himself enthusiastically described them in the first production: "the attack on the hill, the falling of the English troops, Warren's half ascending the hill, and animating the Americans, the smoke and confusion, altogether produce an effect scarce credible."[11] Though *The Battle of Bunker Hill* was Sollee's biggest hit, not every member of the audience was pleased with its clumsy devices of allegory, symbolism, and patriotic rhetoric. "I last night saw Mrs. Merry's Juliet with much delight," wrote William Dunlap in his diary, "whilst Bunkers Hill was performing to a mere rabble . . . and even they execrated it."[12]

At the Greenwich Street Theatre, Wignell offered a solid classical repertory, based heavily on Shakespeare, but not to be outdone, he also presented for one performance Thomas Morton's historical play *Columbus*, which boasted not only a grand procession of Indians and the sacrifice of an Indian maiden, but also a raging volcano and an earthquake.

As the stand at the John Street Theatre stretched on through September, Sollee's business fell disastrously. He found himself "in debt to everybody,"[13] and he was finally forced to announce his closing. He managed to keep playing into early October, however, and Eliza and the rest of the company must have had some pleasure and excitement in giving their closing performance, *The Battle of Bunker Hill,* with President John Adams in the audience. They could not have been pleased with his reaction to the play, however. At the end of the play, while Giles Barrett, one of Sollee's leading actors, was escorting the president to his carriage, Adams abruptly turned to him and said: "My friend General Warren was a scholar and a gentleman, but your author has made him a bully and a blackguard!"[14]

Sollee gave Eliza, her mother, and Tubbs advances for their transportation,[15] and along with the other actors they set sail for Charleston while Wignell's company continued to do good business at the Greenwich Street Theatre into November.

4

# The Charleston Comedians

CHARLESTON, SOUTH CAROLINA, closely resembled a gracious and opulent European city, and when Eliza arrived there, it was at the height of a prosperity brought on by the rice, indigo, and cotton fortunes from the great plantations of the Ashley and Cooper Rivers, at whose mouths the city of Charleston lay before its sprawling harbor.

Charleston was a planter's city, and over half of the population were black slaves. The abundance of slaves and the semitropical climate made life easier, and Eliza found that the carriages moved more slowly than they had in New York or Boston, and they even made less noise in the narrow, sandy streets.

Enormous and elegant mansions fronted the bay. Among the planters' many townhouses Eliza saw the unique Charleston singlehouses, built with the gable end toward the street, only one room wide, and a long, shady piazza running the length of the house. All the buildings were low and spread apart, providing room for the air to circulate, and these spaces were filled with vacant lots or "greens," as they were called, and luxuriant gardens. In the coastal low country surrounding the city and harbor were cypress swamps, palmetto trees, and ancient live oaks covered with low-hanging Spanish moss.

The population was of English, Scottish, French, and African extraction. And as the black hucksters sold their wares in the open-air markets and along King Street, Eliza heard the Charleston patois, Gullah, a language in itself derived from the English, French, and African dialects of its populace.[1]

Despite its distance from the northern cities, Charleston was far from a provincial southern city. The planters' sons had been educated in England. The College of Charleston, the St. Cecilia Society, and the Charleston Library Society were all established institutions, and from the early eighteenth century Charlestonians had been avid theatregoers.[2] Eliza would face as knowledgeable and sophisticated a public there as existed in any city in the United States.

Her engagement at Charleston's City Theatre[3] began unfortunately with a disappointment. With a few exceptions the company that Sollee brought to the City Theatre was the same that he had had at the John Street Theatre in New York. The Barretts, however, who had returned to Boston, were replaced by Alexandre Placide and his wife Charlotte. For the opening night on 7 November

Sollee chose *The Spoiled Child* as the afterpiece, and though he had cast Eliza in Hartford and New York in the role of Maria in this play, he replaced her in Charleston with Charlotte Placide. Instead of appearing in the company's opening, therefore, Eliza had to be content with quietly and inconspicuously making her Charleston debut a little over a week later singing "The Market Lass."

Opportunities for her to appear before the Charleston public were to come slowly, but there did follow three small assignments for her in the two weeks after her debut. She played the Page in James Cross's *The Purse* and the Boy in Samuel Birch's *The Adopted Child.* Both of these short afterpieces were billed as "musical dramas." They were neatly and crisply written and played before swiftly changing scenery. Eliza had songs in both of them and several good short scenes. Her third assignment was her first Shakespearean role, the Duke of York in *Richard III.*

These roles were all valuable additions to her repertoire, but they were small. Eighteenth-century playwrights wrote many excellent parts for children, for the apprentice system prevailed, and actors began their training early. Often, though, in a strong company the best children's roles went to an experienced actress. This was the case in Sollee's company, for both Mrs. Williamson and Mrs. Placide had children's parts in their repertoires, and consequently Eliza had to be content with playing infrequently.

The day after Christmas she did play Cupid in the pantomime *The Magic Chamber,* both her mother and Tubbs appearing with her, and when the company moved the few blocks down Broad Street to the more spacious Charleston Theatre, she appeared once more as a walk-on in *The Battle of Bunker Hill,* as she had in New York, and for the second time in Charleston she played the Boy in *The Adopted Child.*

The company must have looked forward to playing the rest of the season at the Charleston Theatre. It was more spacious and better designed than the City Theatre; it seated over a thousand and had a large circular apron fronting the proscenium. Sollee redecorated it before his opening there, but scarcely had his company played two weeks in this new home than the damage caused by a backstage fire made it necessary for them to move back to the City Theatre until repairs were made. This was an unwelcome move for the actors, for the City Theatre had been converted from a large brick building on Church Street, and though it had been remodeled by Sollee in the course of its use, it was not a proper theatre.

Here Eliza appeared briefly as Mrs. Whitlock's son in Southerne's poetic tragedy *Isabella,* and she danced in an extravagant "musical and allegorical masque" written by a citizen of Charleston and rather fancifully titled *Americania and Eleutheria.* Eliza was a dancing nymph; Tubbs also danced; and Eliza's mother played Vesperia, the chief attendant on Americania. The characters included great winged spirits and satyrs, and even Lucifer put in an appearance.

It was all in celebration of the American Revolution, a cause still close to the hearts of the audience, and the plot centered around the meeting of Americania, the genius of America, with Eleutheria, the goddess of liberty. Audiences of Eliza's day loved this kind of spectacle and allegory.

After a month in its smaller quarters the company moved back to the Charleston Theatre, where Eliza was cast as Julia in Henry Siddons's *The Sicilian Romance*. This was to be her last and most important assignment in Sollee's company. Though Julia is a secondary role, she appears throughout the play and has very good scenes and even a soliloquy.

Meantime, as the end of the season approached, trouble was brewing in the company. Eliza herself could not have become directly involved in the bitter disputes that were developing, nor could she have known when the squabbling first started what important opportunities would come her way as a result. But she would certainly have heard the details of the grievances, because her testy stepfather, Charles Tubbs, was in the thick of the fighting.[4]

Unlike his wife, who had been given excellent assignments by Sollee in both New York and Charleston, Tubbs had had to content himself with a decidedly secondary place as an actor, performing mostly in that frustrating category that managers even then called "useful actors," and he was consistently cast in the dull but necessary parts of any repertory that are inevitably the lot of useful actors. For him this had been a humiliating comedown from his experience as a manager and leading actor of the New England tour, and he had grown resentful. He needed to assert himself, and the opportunity soon came.

As the season drew to a close, benefits were announced, and suddenly the "imperious Mrs. Whitlock," as Sollee later called her in one of his many statements to the press, in a dispute over salary, refused to play her benefit. The Whitlocks maintained that the management was late in paying their salaries. They were quickly joined in their complaint by a number of other members of the company including Charles Tubbs, Tubbs claiming that when he had gone personally to Sollee and asked for his, Eliza's, and Mrs. Tubbs's salaries (together they came to $43.00), the manager had threatened to bring an action of damages against him, warning him that he was a stranger in Charleston, would not be able to find bail, and in such case probably be taken to prison.

The group of actors claiming not to have been paid demanded their pay immediately. Sollee refused, contending that the salaries they demanded were not unduly late, and that anyway most of the actors owed him their travel expenses, including Tubbs who was also in his debt for a bill of $38.00 to cover Tubbs's, his wife's, and Eliza's board in Hartford.

The dissatisfied actors retaliated by publishing playbills stating that the leading actors would no longer be playing at the Charleston Theatre, and that evening at the theatre the announcement of the necessary last-minute change in bill was hissed.

Enraged, Sollee took his cause to the press. Tubbs was a *vermin*. Moreover, he was a thief, since he had taken from the theatre's wardrobe "the Harlequin dress [Tubbs had played Harlequin in *The Magic Chamber*] and some boys clothes made for Miss Arnold." The Messrs. Whitlock and Edgar, whom Sollee singled out with bitter resentment, were ringleaders in a conspiracy against him. Edgar (who was soon to assume an important role in Eliza's career) was not only the culprit who had hissed the announcement of the change in bill, he was not even a member of the company, because he had been fired "having been intoxicated and unable to perform for three nights running without being hissed."

It was a donnybrook. The newspapers were besieged with opinions from management, actors, and public alike over the controversy.[5]

Sollee had been under difficult financial pressure all year, and earlier that season there had also been a staggering blow to his future plans as a manager. Not long after the small fire at the Charleston Theatre, news had reached him that on 3 February the Federal Street Theatre in Boston had burned to the ground. This virtually ended the Boston-Charleston exchange for which he had such great hopes. After much black print and bickering in the Charleston papers, Sollee was forced to resign, ending his career as a manager and relinquishing the management of the company remaining at the Charleston Theatre to three of the actors who had remained loyal to him throughout the dispute: Alexandre Placide, John Williamson, and Edgar Jones.

Meantime, the actors who had left Sollee's company immediately set about planning to organize their own management, and in the interim a group of them, including Tubbs, his wife, and Eliza, went up the coast to Wilmington, North Carolina, where they played for nine nights.[6] Eliza was barnstorming again as she had in New England, but in the smaller company she had the opportunity to play more often. From the only record of this short engagement in Wilmington, it is known that she added at least one important new part to her repertoire, and that was Norah in John O'Keefee's comic opera *The Poor Soldier*. She must also have played some of the roles she had in New England, performing as a singer and dancer as well.

Back in Charleston, Placide, Williamson, and Jones, succeeding Sollee in management, continued their season through the end of March, when they took their company down the coast to play a short season in Savannah.[7] By this time the actors who had left Sollee's company had formed their own management, and they now moved into the Charleston Theatre to open a short engagement on 9 April.

Returning from their stand in Wilmington, Eliza, her mother, and Tubbs all joined this company, which called itself the Charleston Comedians and was under the leadership of the irascible and (according to Sollee's opinion) ungrateful and intemperate Edgar.[8]

Sollee's opinion notwithstanding, Edgar played an important part in Eliza's career, for he cast her as his leading ingenue. In doing this he was the first manager outside of her family to bring her forward in a company of seasoned actors. Harper, in Providence and Newport, had cast her well but infrequently; Sollee had used her even less frequently; but Edgar not only billed her as an important member of his company and kept her very busy, he also cast her in far more important and challenging roles.

Once again, as she had in New England, Eliza plunged into a heavy rehearsal and performance schedule. On the opening night of the Charleston Comedians she was in both short plays that were the afterpieces. She played Biddy Belair in *Miss in Her Teens* and also a part new to her repertoire, Nancy in Thomas Murphy's farce *Three Weeks after Marriage.* As both Nancy and Biddy, eleven-year-old Eliza was pursued by lovers, including the inevitable fops, and insisted, like all heroines of sentimental comedy, on marrying for love, and as she explained in the part of Nancy, "not for card playing."

Two nights after the opening, when the Whitlocks played the leading roles in Schiller's melodrama *Intrigue and Love,* Edgar chose *The Spoiled Child* for the afterpiece and at last gave Eliza the opportunity to appear as Little Pickle for the Charleston public. In doing so, the eleven-year-old girl was facing formidable competition, for Charleston had last seen Mrs. Williamson in the role.

Eliza's next important role was Pink in John O'Keefee's comedy *The Young Quaker.* This was her first assignment in a line of parts that was to become very important in her repertoire. Pink is one of those wise, earthy, and intriguing maids that appear throughout the eighteenth-century repertory. This line of parts was often called soubrette, from the French *soubret,* meaning coy. Eliza would eventually excel in them. Edgar also used her often as a singer and dancer, and during the final week of his season he gave her a benefit with her stepfather. In the first play on her benefit night she played Sophia in Thomas Holcroft's sturdily sentimental play *The Road to Ruin.* This is an excellent part and one of the two leading women's roles in the play. In the afterpiece Eliza played Phoebe in *Rosina* with her mother in the title role, and since this was her final important appearance of the season, she came out during one of the interludes and spoke the farewell address that had been written for her in Portland.

The Charleston Comedians closed the first of May. For Eliza it had been an important engagement. She had stepped squarely into the professional world.

# 5

# A Legacy

IT WAS AN ADULT WORLD that eleven-year-old Eliza had entered. For the rest of her life she would continually face the constant pressure of survival in a highly competitive profession in which work opportunities were seasonal and scarce. In order to survive as an actress, she would have to build a large and useful repertoire, and, most important of all, she would have to find work and become known to the public.

She did not yet have to face these responsibilities alone, however, for after the closing of the Charleston Comedians in the summer of 1798, her immediate future still lay in the hands of her mother and her stepfather.

After closing in Charleston, Charles Tubbs, as head of the family, considered his next move. It can hardly be said that his own standing in the profession he had so recently adopted was good. He had not been successful as a manager in New England, and his short career as an actor had been discouraging. Though he had managed to find some employment, mostly through his wife's connections, he had unfortunately managed to get himself involved in serious disputes with both managers with whom he had worked. Moreover, news from the North was discouraging. The Academy Theatre in Richmond and the Federal Street Theatre in Boston had both burned that season, and there was little chance for work in the other northern cities, because it was already summer and most of the theatres were closed.

What seemed the most likely and, indeed, the closest prospect where Tubbs could seek work for himself, his wife, and Eliza was Thomas Wade West's Virginia Company, which played a year-round circuit that included Norfolk, Petersburg, Fredericksburg, Alexandria, and Richmond.

It was a long trip to Virginia through North Carolina, but there were towns along the way where, Tubbs planned, they could present concerts and short plays as they had in New England and more recently in Wilmington. Before leaving Charleston, he arranged a concert for 2 May, in which both Eliza and her mother sang, and then shortly after they all three set out for Virginia through the small towns along the inlets and rivers that laced the inner banks of the North Carolina coast.

By mid-July they had made their way to Halifax, North Carolina, a small town on the Roanoke River, just south of the Virginia state line.[1] Some of the actors with whom they had recently worked in Charleston must have been with them, because they billed themselves in the papers as the Charleston Comedians and announced that their performances would be in Col. Tabbs Tavern, where they had also taken rooms.

Almost immediately, however, they were forced to change their plans, because Eliza's mother (she was most likely the small company's leading actress) became ill, and performances had to be postponed. Mrs. Tubbs was well enough to play again after a week's rest, and on 23 July the *North Carolina Journal* announced that she would be featured as Maria in *The Citizen,* a part she had also played in New England. This is the last record of a performance by Eliza's mother, and the absence of her name from the subsequent records probably means that the illness she had contracted in the hot summer climate during the long trip through North Carolina was fatal.[2]

Since her illness coincided with a yellow-fever epidemic that was then plaguing the east coast of the United States, it could have been this disease that caused her death. With alarming speed the epidemic had spread: Portsmouth, New London, New York, Philadelphia, Baltimore, and into parts of Virginia and North Carolina. In the panic that followed its outbreak, thousands evacuated the cities and towns, taking to the country in an attempt to escape infection. Fear of contagion was widespread. Houses were boarded up, and strangers were suspect and unwelcome, for they brought with them the threat of disease and death. It was under this shadow that Tubbs and his family had made their trip through North Carolina, uncertain of how the epidemic would affect their lives, not knowing what prospects they had either of finding audiences for a concert or of landing an engagement, because at the first word of the dreaded fever, public gatherings were prohibited and the theatres always closed.[3]

To a child the death of a parent is a puzzling and frightening shock, and for Eliza it was especially so, for she and her mother had lived and worked very closely together. But what probably was even more unsettling to the young girl was that her mother's death meant that she was now left entirely in the care of her stepfather, who more than once since his marriage to her mother had shown himself to be a temperamental and unstable man. It must have been a confusing time for Eliza as she traveled toward Richmond with him, the memory of her mother's death a constant reminder of the danger of infection that still lay in every tavern, boarding house, and strange new town.

Further to the north, the Virginia Company, under the management of Thomas Wade West, had spent most of the summer in Fredericksburg, safe from the fever.[4] After closing a very long ten-week season there in mid-October, West's company traveled south to Petersburg,[5] where it usually played an engagement during the fall, afterward moving back north the short distance to Rich-mond.

It was during this time that Tubbs, either by audition or some previous correspondence, succeeded in obtaining an engagement with West for both himself and Eliza, because when the Virginia Company began its Richmond season in the temporary theatre in the Market Hall, both their names appear in the bills.[6]

Eliza was to spend most of this winter with Tubbs in Richmond. She was safe from the fever there and back at work again in a company in which there were children her own age. The nucleus of West's company was his own family and that of his brother-in-law, Matthew Sully. Many of the West and Sully children (including Thomas Sully, the painter) appeared in the Virginia Company as actors. That winter, for the first time, Eliza met Margaret West; her daughter, the greatly admired Anne West; William Green and his wife Hope Green; and Matthew Sully, Jr., a boy of Eliza's own age, who like her was just beginning his apprenticeship. She would come to know them all well and work with them many times throughout her career.

For her debut in Richmond on 10 December, Eliza was cast as Trusty in John Vanbrugh's comedy *The Provoked Husband*.[7] Trusty was new to her repertoire, a short but important soubrette role, and most of her scenes were with the Virginia Company's leading lady, the excellent comedienne Anne West, daughter of Thomas Wade West and Margaret Sully West.

The Wests were an extraordinarily talented family. They had presented their first season in Richmond in 1790 at the old Academy Theatre and, joined by the Sullys, in the ensuing eight years had succeeded in establishing a circuit that gave their company year-round employment. Under the leadership of Thomas Wade West they had managed to build new theatres by subscription in Norfolk, Petersburg, Alexandria, and Fredericksburg, and though Charleston was no longer on the circuit, they had also built the Charleston Theatre, where Eliza and Tubbs had played the preceding spring. The Wests also enjoyed an enthusiastic public.

Eliza was able to find a place for herself very quickly in the Virginia Company's repertory. The legacy she had received from her mother could scarcely have consisted of a great deal of money or possessions, but it was nonetheless a very tangible one. In the short and intense apprenticeship under her guidance, Eliza had received excellent training. She had learned and developed a repertoire that was very useful to a theatrical manager, and this was a stroke of very good fortune, because it would give her life direction at a time when she sorely needed it.

Although West was able to cast her immediately into his repertory, there were some problems in using her frequently. The boys' roles, or "breeches parts," that she had played so well in Charleston and New England were assigned to

Matthew Sully, Jr., who was about her age, and even though she could and did play some soubrette and ingenue roles, she was still slightly young to be cast very often in either of these lines. With employment conditions as they were, however, both she and Tubbs were fortunate to have jobs, and they undoubtedly counted their blessings.

It was not long, however, before Eliza was to land a key engagement that was to be the most important opportunity yet to come her way, and thanks to her mother's training, she was ready for it.

# The Chestnut Street Theatre

MEANTIME, the yellow fever epidemic had continued throughout the cities in the middle states. Philadelphia was the worst hit. The pestilence, as the people came to call it, raged there for nearly four months, claiming well over three thousand lives, or nearly five percent of the population. At the height of the epidemic the daily death toll rose to over one hundred, as authorities implored the citizens to evacuate. The city itself was a nightmare. Its wide streets were all but abandoned except for the death carts, and virtually all business ceased. Only the Health Office remained open night and day for the gruesome task of burying the dead.[1]

It was not until early February 1799 that the epidemic finally subsided in Philadelphia, and it was safe for Thomas Wignell, manager of the Chestnut Street Theatre there, to reassemble his company and begin planning to open a belated season.

Eliza and Tubbs both had connections with Wignell. They had worked with the Whitlocks, who were closely associated with him, and some of the actors who were based at the Chestnut Street Theatre had known Eliza's mother in England. Moreover, the close proximity of the Virginia Company's circuit to Philadelphia made for a great deal of exchange between these two companies.[2] There was ample opportunity, therefore, for Tubbs to bring Eliza to Wignell's attention.

And Wignell was interested in her. He had had the opportunity of seeing her during the fall of 1797 in one of her brief appearances at the John Street Theatre in New York; and he would also have known of her work in New England, Charleston, and with the Virginia Company. But most important of all, Eliza's repertoire of some twenty-five parts, a repertoire that in the last three years she had learned under her mother's careful guidance, was a valuable asset to him. As a child actress she could be cast well and frequently. Wignell hired her and began planning to introduce her to the Philadelphia public in some of her best vehicles. This was to be Eliza's most important engagement yet, and it meant that she would be playing with one of the most distinguished companies in the country. It was also to be a crucial turn in her life, for it marked the beginning of her independence from Charles Tubbs. If he, too, applied for work in Phila-

delphia with Wignell, he was unsuccessful. Evidently his reputation was beginning to catch up with him, because Wignell did not hire him.


Thomas Wignell was the son of an actor in Garrick's company, and when he
hired Eliza, he was at the height of his career.[3] He had joined the old American
Company as a sharing actor, or stockholder, and after his American debut in
1785 he had established himself as a popular comedian, enjoying the distinction
of being a personal favorite of George Washington. One of his most important
successes was Jonathan in Royall Tyler's *The Contrast,* a part he created. In a
dispute over management he had left the American Company and with Alexander Reinagle, the English composer and conductor, had founded and built the
Chestnut Street Theatre in Philadelphia, where as a manager he introduced to
American audiences many of the finest actors of his time including James
Fennell, Thomas Cooper, William Warren, Elizabeth Kemble Whitlock, and
Ann Merry. Many of Wignell's contemporaries called his company the finest
America had seen, and all of them spoke of it with the highest regard.

The theatre in which he housed his large company and staff was at Chestnut
and Sixth Streets, just opposite Congress Hall and very near Independence Hall.
To a later audience this theatre would come to be known as "Old Drury," but
when Eliza first came to Philadelphia in early 1799, it was called the New
Theatre, and though it was already five years old, its exterior was still unfinished.
It was nonetheless a large and elegantly designed house with marble stairways
leading to two tiers of handsomely gilt boxes. Like most eighteenth-century
playhouses, it also had a gallery and a large pit with circular, backless benches. It
would be the largest theatre in which Eliza had yet played, for when it was filled,
it held two thousand, a large house by any standards and exceptional for its day.
The stage was thirty-six feet wide and seventy-one feet deep, and it was one of
the best equipped with scenery in the country.[4]


Based on what reports she had heard while he was in Virginia, Eliza would
have envisioned Philadelphia as an exhausted and plague-ridden city suffering
under the ravages of the yellow fever. But when she arrived there in January
1799, all traces of the epidemic had disappeared. She found instead a sprawling
and beautiful metropolis, the largest city in the United States, covering twice
the ground of Boston, flanked on the east and west by the Delaware and
Schuylkill Rivers, with broad streets neatly laid out at right angles, and ample,
paved sidewalks lined at regular intervals with street lamps and hitching posts.

The year Eliza arrived, Philadelphia was still the capital of the United States,
and one was accustomed to seeing the nation's leaders and founders in public
places there. On her way to the theatre, next to Congress Hall, she would pass
senators and representatives from all of the sixteen states, and in the boarding

house or tavern in which she lodged, she probably met many French refugees, some of them from the French Revolution, others from the slave rebellion in Santo Domingo. In the arcaded marketplace on High Street or in the tree-lined squares, she could still see some Quakers, dressed in their plain and somber garb, but even though they were the oldest citizens, to her they would have looked like strangers in the motley crowds that surrounded them.

During an age of soubriquets Philadelphia was often called the "Athens of America."[5] In 1799 Washington's elegant republican court had ended, and John Adams was the president. Adams was a New Englander with less extravagant tastes than his illustrious predecessor, but during his administration federal officials as well as emissaries of foreign governments still maintained an active and brilliant social life with the rich Philadelphia shippers and merchants, and theatregoing was very much an important part of it.

The complete shutdown of the Chestnut Street Theatre during the epidemic had whetted the public's appetite for plays, and when its season reopened on 5 February, crowds began flocking to see the repertory. The actors were back, and in the excitement and enthusiasm that came with the large audiences Eliza, as a new member of the company, could hear the older actors joking about how their long-time opponents in Philadelphia, the Quakers, believed that the fever and the actors "moved in a perpetual circle, reproducing each other: the fever, the actors—the actors, the fever!"[6]

The season was already late in getting underway, and with the large company—Wignell had forty-three actors under contract that season—it took time for all of them, many of whom had large and popular followings in Philadelphia, to make their first appearances of the season. Accordingly, Eliza's debut did not take place until 18 March.

Wignell decided to introduce her to Philadelphia audiences as Biddy Belair in Garrick's farce *Miss in Her Teens,* as a comedienne rather than a singing actress. This was the same vehicle in which she had made her debuts both in Portland and with the Charleston Comedians, and a role that her mother had first prepared her for two years earlier in Portland.

Appearing as Eliza's suitors in this play were two of the Chestnut Street Theatre's leading comedians. Wignell himself played Captain Flash, the braggart soldier, and John Bernard, a prominent Covent Garden actor whom Wignell had recently brought to America, was the fop Fribble (a part that Garrick had made famous). As Biddy Belair, Eliza was in the role that in Garrick's day had been played by the legendary Kitty Clive.

At twelve Eliza was younger than Biddy, who in the play is a sixteen-year-old "young lady of wit, beauty, and fifteen thousand pounds fortune."[7] Nontheles, her precocious appeal fitted the part well, and the success she had already enjoyed as Biddy would have given her some confidence in facing the new audience. And she needed confidence in beginning her first season in Wignell's company. Her mother was no longer there to give her support and help, and without even Tubbs in the company Eliza now had to begin making her way as an actress very much on her own.

Wignell was a generous manager, and in presenting her to his public he took care that she had the opportunity of showing the full range of her repertoire. After her debut her next assignments were both "breeches" parts, or parts in which she would have worn tights and—in a day of long dresses—given the audience a good look at her legs. This was a popular device that few clever actresses could resist and perhaps even fewer curious audiences would have failed to enjoy. It was important that she play these parts, so she appeared as the obstreperous Little Pickle in *The Spoiled Child* and then as the milder and more obedient Boy in *The Adopted Child.* Both of these roles were very different from Biddy Belair, and in both of them Eliza had excellent songs. She then danced in the pantomime *Highland Festivity,* created by the Chestnut Street Theatre's choreographer, Oscar Byrne. There followed a number of other assignments including an appearance as Norah in *The Poor Soldier,* in which she was Wignell's leading lady. It was a busy season for her.

For her benefit, on 29 April, Wignell cast her as Moggy McGilpin in John O'Keeffe's *The Highland Reel.* Whimsical, spritely, good-hearted, and hardheaded, Moggy is an excellent character for a clever comedienne. She has very funny scenes and charming songs. Actresses many years Eliza's senior enjoyed great success in the part and often played it, among them Mrs. Oldmixon and Mrs. Williamson (who had created the role in the play's premiere in London). Moggy McGilpin was also to become an important part of Eliza's repertoire, and she would play it successfully throughout her career. This was her first time in the role.

A young actress cannot always choose her parts, and consequently her early development depends more often than not on casting decisions made by others. Until now Eliza's mother had to a great extent been able to make these decisions for her, carefully guiding the growth of Eliza's repertoire, finding work for her, coaching her in roles she herself had played, bringing her a long way toward becoming a full-fledged professional able to compete for roles in any company. But now Eliza's mother was gone. Tubbs remained, uncertain, unpredictable, and thoroughly unsuited by either training or temperament to fill the place in Eliza's life left empty by her mother's death. He had brought her to Philadelphia and would still remain with her for a short while, but he could never become for her a parental figure toward whom she looked for guidance and support. If Eliza needed an anchor upon which to secure the disquieting emotions of an adolescent adjusting not only to the loss of her only parent but also to the growing pressures of a hectic and demanding professional life, she would have had to look to someone other than her stepfather.

Perhaps it was Thomas Wignell who began to fill this place in her life. He was certainly showing a keen personal interest in her development as an actress. He consistently cast her well throughout her first season in Philadelphia, and he offered her a return engagement for the following season, which she accepted.[8]

Wignell kept his actors busy nearly all year. Immediately after closing in Philadelphia, he always moved his company to the Holliday Street Theatre in Baltimore, and after a short early summer season there the company usually toured the nearby towns during the rest of the summer (Annapolis, Georgetown, Alexandria, or the small towns along the Delaware), eventually returning to Baltimore for a longer season in the early fall before going back home to Philadelphia for the regular season at the Chestnut Street Theatre. During this time on tour away from Philadelphia, Wignell often gave the younger members of his company the opportunity of trying out new parts,[9] and in Baltimore he assigned six new roles to Eliza, all different enough to require a wide range and versatility on her part. In most of them she sang. Her new roles ranged from the rustic maid Molly Maybush in John O'Keeffee's *The Farmer* (in which she had to master a country dialect) to the dashing young soldier Prince John in Shakespeare's *Henry IV, Part 1*. Besides these new parts she also had the chance to play again some of the roles she had learned in Philadelphia that spring. She was also dancing, and often prominently, in the company's repertoire of ballets and pantomimes.[10]

Tubbs seems still to have been with her, though what her precise relationship to him was at this time it is impossible to say. He did make a brief appearance on her benefit night in Baltimore that fall, but his name never appears in any other connection with Wignell's company, and the advertisement listing him as the Master of the Hotel in Thomas Holcroft's *He's Much to Blame* is the last document that definitely ties him to Eliza.[11] No doubt she was depending on him less and less. By now she was certainly earning a salary with which she could support herself, and the interest Wignell was showing in her was beginning to give her a very strong foothold in the profession for which her mother had begun training her four years earlier. By the time she had ended her first season in Philadelphia, whatever fears she may have had about a future with Charles Tubbs must have begun to dissolve. It was apparent that she no longer had to rely on him. She could earn her living as an actress, completely on her own.

When Eliza began her second season at the Chestnut Street Theatre, she was barely thirteen, and she was beginning to blossom into a very beautiful young woman with delicate features, abundant curling hair, and large, brown, glowing eyes. Her figure was small and graceful, as it was to remain for the rest of her life, and this was to prove an advantage for her, because it meant that she could continue to play children's parts while she was growing into an ingenue and young leading lady. Her repertoire was to expand considerably during this season,[12] and since her skills as actress, singer, and dancer suited her especially well for the comic operas, it was in these plays that Wignell began casting her most frequently.

Comic operas, as Eliza's contemporaries called them, were not operas in the strictest sense, but the eighteenth-century equivalent of the modern musical, and they flourished in England and America during the latter half of the eighteenth century. They had developed from the earlier ballad operas in which the playwright used popular airs, tunes, or ballads for his songs but wrote the words for the songs himself. The familiar melodies in the context of the plays had a humorous and ironic effect for the audiences. By Eliza's day, however, ballad operas had run their course, and they were far less popular than the newer comic operas, which all had original scores. Audiences loved the comic operas, and they were an important part of every theatre's repertory.[13]

Early in Eliza's second season with Wignell's company George Washington died at Mount Vernon. Washington's death profoundly affected every citizen of the young country, because he was a national hero in every sense of the word, and Eliza could not have failed to have been deeply impressed with the grief that many of her fellow actors felt, especially the older ones. There was good reason for this, because the nation's first president had been an enthusiastic theatregoer, and this had helped actors enormously in their long struggle for respectability. Indeed, many actors at the Chestnut Street Theatre could remember when President Washington had gone to the theatre in Philadelphia even though an old Quaker law prohibiting plays had still been on the books. Eliza took part in the memorial service that the actors gave at the theatre. It was a solemn occasion, and she stood onstage with the entire company, all of them dressed in black. There was music specially composed for this memorial, and Wignell, who had been a favorite of Washington's, spoke the eulogy.[14]

After closing to observe a period of mourning, the theatre reopened, and Eliza returned to a busy work schedule again playing Little Pickle, Moggy McGilpin, Prince John, and some of the roles she had learned on tour during the summer. She also began rehearsing and performing a number of new ones.

At mid-season a young man named Charles Hopkins arranged to make his debut as an actor at the Chestnut Street Theatre. It was the first time he had ever appeared onstage, and as was customary, he billed himself anonymously as "a young gentleman." Wignell, as was also customary, cast him in a substantial role, giving him a fair and ruthless exposure to the public. Hopkins played one of the most famous comic roles of that or any other time, Tony Lumpkin in Oliver Goldsmith's *She Stoops to Conquer,* and his debut was enormously successful.[15] Wignell recognized him immediately as a born comedian and character actor and offered him an engagement for the rest of the season.

Eliza saw a great deal of Charles Hopkins that spring, for Wignell kept them both very busy. They were often cast in the same plays, and their lives centered on rehearsals and performances at the large theatre on Chestnut Street. There was little time for either of them to do anything else. Eliza, at thirteen, was the more highly trained and experienced, but Charles's instincts were sure and strong, and Wignell advanced him quickly.

Not long after Charles's debut, Thomas Cooper began a special engagement at the Chestnut Street Theatre. Handsome, eccentric, and capricious, Cooper was twenty-four and just on the verge of being recognized as the leading tragic actor in America. His engagement meant that the Philadelphia public could see more of its great favorite Ann Merry, who in the absence of a strong leading man in the company that season had been unable to play many of her famous tragic roles. Charles and Eliza were both given assignments to play in support of these two brilliant actors. Although Eliza had already frequently appeared with Mrs. Merry, this was her first association with Cooper, but she would work with him again, and under vastly different circumstances.

When the season ended in Philadelphia, Charles and Eliza traveled with the company to Baltimore and the Holliday Street Theatre, where after playing a shorter season than usual, they shared a benefit. They then set out for the new federal city of Washington (it was a nine-hour trip from Baltimore by coach), where they looked forward to playing in the first season at the new theatre there.

Plans for building the new capitol city had been underway for a decade, but when Eliza and Charles arrived there from Baltimore in the summer of 1800, they found that Washington was little more than a sprawling village set in beautiful natural surroundings on the wide banks of the Potomac. Its buildings were widespread and mostly incomplete, many of them surrounded with stone, lumber, debris, and the clutter of workmen. The President's Mansion (not yet called the White House) was nearly completed, but the new Capitol building had only its north wing standing. Between the two stretched Pennsylvania Avenue, lined with elder bushes, swamp grass, and tree stumps. The population of the federal city was 3,210, including slaves and freed Negroes, smaller still than either of the nearby towns of Georgetown and its environs or Alexandria.[16]

Removal of the seat of the national government to Washington had begun in May of that year, and Wignell had been invited to present his company in a temporary theatre there at the Lottery Hotel. He had responded with great enthusiasm to this proposal, and he had spared no expense in preparing new scenery and decor. When he arrived with his company from Baltimore, however, it was already late summer, and many of the government officials, including President Adams, were away. Congress was not to convene until November. To some it may have seemed an inauspicious time and place to present a theatrical season, but Wignell and his company saw it differently. For them it was the opportunity of establishing a theatre at the very center of their young country's national life. Unfortunately, however, they were unable to open as planned, because the new scenery that Wignell had ordered was severely damaged in a rainstorm on its way from Philadelphia, and the resulting repairs and repainting made it necessary to set the opening night forward to 22 August.

Charles and Eliza would not have missed the sense of occasion that filled the small theatre in the Lottery Hotel on that evening. It was the opening of Washington's first theatre, and they were taking part in a historic event. Wignell spoke a humorous prologue in verse explaining the reasons for the delay in the opening,[17] and there followed a performance of Thomas Otway's verse tragedy *Venice Preserved* with a distinguished company headed by Thomas Cooper, Thomas Wignell, Ann Merry, William Wood, and William Warren. Charles appeared in the supporting role of Elliot, and following the tragedy, Eliza had the distinction of playing the leading role of Little Pickle in the farce.

The season at the Lottery Hotel continued for four weeks, during which Eliza and Charles both appeared regularly. It was during this season that Eliza added another important new part to her repertoire when she played Priscilla Tomboy in Isaac Bickerstaffe's *The Romp*. Like Little Pickle and Moggy McGilpin, this was to become one of her most successful vehicles. *The Romp* is a farce, written very much in the style of *The Spoiled Child*, and the role of the hoydenish Priscilla demands a sprightly and athletic performance with plenty of energy, vitality, and bad temper. There are also excellent songs and ample opportunity for inventive business. Eliza knew the play well, having already played the smaller role of Penelope in it.

The season ended in mid-September,[18] and the company had to return directly to Philadelphia instead of playing its usual fall season in Baltimore. Business in Washington had been good, and the actors had been well received, but expenses were high and losses heavy, and Wignell and his company had to accept the unwelcome fact that the establishment of a permanent theatre in Washington (there was already talk of a national theatre) would have to wait.

Eliza and Charles had both agreed to return to the Chestnut Street Theatre for the regular season in Philadelphia. It would be her third season in Wignell's company and his second. By now both of them were cast well into the repertory, and they played frequently, Eliza most often appearing in the comic operas and afterpieces. Wignell was beginning to cast her in some parts as a young leading lady, but her figure and age still restricted the number of roles for which she was right. With Charles, however, it was a different matter. Not only were there always more roles for men than for women, but he also had another advantage. He had a flair for character acting that stretched his range beyond that of most young actors. Wignell had been able to cast him constantly ever since his debut, and he had played a great many new parts, very often appearing in both the main play and the afterpiece on the same evening. It is true that he was most often in secondary roles, but his repertoire was developing very quickly, and in a short time he was on his way toward building an excellent reputation for himself.

Eliza and Charles were seeing more and more of each other. Rehearsals and performances brought them together day and night, and there was little time for either of them to make friends outside the small world in which they lived and worked. They were both young and attractive, and they shared the same interests. What was more natural than that they should fall in love?[19]

When that season ended in March, Eliza had added ten new roles to her repertoire.[20] It had been her busiest Philadelphia season yet. Both she and Charles then moved with the company to Baltimore, and since they had not played at the Holliday Street Theatre the preceding fall, the summer season in Baltimore was longer than usual, lasting from late April to early June.

Like any young actor worth his salt, Charles was full of energy and ambition, and he wanted to play the great roles. He realized, however, that if he remained with Wignell, this would be impossible. Wignell already had some of the finest actors in the country and having to compete with them for parts would hardly give him the opportunities to tackle the roles he was longing to play. Therefore, when Margaret West offered him an engagement with the Virginia Company for the season of 1801–2, he accepted it. This was exactly the chance he needed, because it meant that he would be playing far more important parts than he could with Wignell. It must have, nonetheless, been a difficult decision for him, because he also knew that it meant that he and Eliza would be separated for the entire next season with little or no chance of seeing each other even for a short visit. She had engagements with a new management in Philadelphia for the rest of the summer and with Wignell for the fall and winter. It must have been an anxious time for them both, and perhaps it was especially so for Eliza. She had to return to the Chestnut Street Theatre where she would be reminded of Charles every day. It would be a lonely time for her. But the decision was made, and after closing at the Holliday Street Theatre in early June, they both left Baltimore, Charles for Virginia and Eliza for Philadelphia. They would be separated for over a year.

On her own again, Eliza began rehearsals in Philadelphia for William Warren's company. It was especially hot that summer.[21] Warren had reopened the old Southwark Theatre, which stood on South Street just outside the Philadelphia city limits (where it had been built in 1766 to avoid any Quaker ordinance prohibiting plays), and he was presenting a season there with a detachment of actors from the Chestnut Street Theatre. This was, of course, with Wignell's permission, because all theatrical managers insisted on exclusive agreements with the actors in their companies.

Eliza had often seen this empty old theatre on South Street, and she had probably heard many of the older actors in Wignell's company speak of playing in it, because it had a long and distinguished history.[22] It had been built as a replica of the John Street Theatre in New York and was in use for over half a century. The Southwark had seen its days of glory when Eliza began rehearsals there, but she could take some pride in knowing that it was in this venerable old house that she would soon appear in the most challenging role she had yet attempted. It would also be her first time in one of the truly great roles, because Warren had cast her as Ophelia in Shakespeare's *Hamlet.*

William Warren (who was to spend his entire career at the Chestnut Street Theatre, eventually becoming co-manager there with William Wood) knew Eliza's work well and had often appeared with her. He had played her father, Old Pickle, in *The Spoiled Child,* and in the closeness of a repertory company he had had the chance to observe her work and growth carefully, realizing that she was capable of giving sensitive portrayals of a kind far removed from the characters generally assigned to her. That he would cast her in this coveted part means that he thought very highly of her indeed. It was a rare opportunity for Eliza, because Ophelia was one of Mrs. Merry's roles, and there was practically no chance of any other actress in Wignell's company playing it during the regular season at the Chestnut Street Theatre.

The season at the Southwark began in mid-August, the old theatre "fitted up for the occasion and rendered as cool as possible"[23] against the late summer heat. As rehearsals and performances progressed and Eliza began studying Ophelia, she found that she was appearing on the same bill with acrobats. Alexandre Placide, whom she had known in Charleston and who had joined Warren as a co-manager for the summer, performed on the tightrope, and a Mr. Robertson, who billed himself as the "Antipodean Whirligig," lived up to his extravagant billing by spinning round on his head "an hundred times a minute." After this dizzying feat he then danced an "egg hornpipe blindfolded among twenty eggs without breaking one of them," and ended his extraordinary act by performing an imitation of birds![24] Such variety was not at all unusual in a theatre during Eliza's day.

It was toward the end of the Southwark season[25] on 23 September that fourteen-year-old Eliza played Ophelia to Alexander Cain's Hamlet, both young actors in these roles for the first time.

An actress's performance vanishes into thin air, living only in the memories of the audiences who see her. Sometimes a contemporary writer or critic can capture something of its brief and fragile life, but even so the performance itself remains at best as elusive as a shadow. Eliza should certainly have brought an innocence and beauty to Ophelia, and her training as a singer and comedienne would have enabled her to give an appropriate lightness and delicacy to the mad scenes, but of her actual performance there is no known record. This was, however, only the beginning of her acquaintance with this difficult and demanding part. She would play it again.

Two weeks after closing at the Southwark, Eliza began her fourth season at the Chestnut Street Theatre.[26] It would be an active, lonely, unsatisfying time for her, and it was marked with a tragedy that touched every actor in Wignell's company very closely.

During the fall and winter weeks a clique formed in Philadelphia against a new actor in the company, John Fullerton. Audiences could be cruel in those days, and poor Fullerton was constantly hissed in the theatre. Anonymous and cutting criticisms of his work appeared in print. The critic from *The Portfolio* even stated openly that Fullerton was simply not entitled to the roles Wignell cast him in.[27] Not all the criticism was hostile, however, and Wignell, who evidently did not agree with Fullerton's critics, continued to cast him in leading parts. But Fullerton was a sensitive man, and he was deeply affected by all the harsh criticism and humiliating demonstrations against him while he was onstage. His spirits sank deeper and deeper. Then one cold night in early February, after dining with Wignell, he returned home to William Francis's house where he boarded. He sat down at the card table to play for a short time, and later that same evening, at about nine o'clock, he took his hat, went out, and drowned himself in the river.[28] The actors must have stood by watching the whole tragic affair in horror, because this was the living nightmare that every one of them feared, and if Eliza herself wondered whether such a critical attack would ever affect her own life, it was a blessing that she could not look into the future.

Fullerton's sudden suicide understandably cast a gloom over the remainder of the season. Business fell, houses were nearly empty, and Wignell was finally obliged to close the theatre for two successive playing nights, an unusual occurrence at the Chestnut Street Theatre.

By now Eliza had become one of Wignell's leading ingenues. She was cast throughout the repertory and could play a number of parts interchangeably in many of the company's popular productions. She was also holding her own with the public, and even the important critic for *The Portfolio* wrote of her "rising excellence."[29] But nonetheless, as Charles had done, she was beginning to realize that further advancement in Wignell's company would be slow for her. She was ready to move on to roles other than those of a singing actress in comic opera and farce, and with Wignell this would be difficult. Her position at the Chestnut Street Theatre could not have been made more plain to her than when Alexander Cain played Hamlet for his benefit at the end of the season, and Mrs. Merry was his Ophelia. Eliza had played Ophelia with Cain herself the preceding summer, but there would be little chance of her getting that kind of assignment at the Chestnut Street Theatre, and she knew it.

Besides, Charles was doing well in Virginia, and she wanted to join him. When the company began its spring season in Baltimore in late April, therefore, she had probably already begun making plans to leave Wignell's company. It was still one of the busiest seasons she had ever had at the Holliday Street Theatre. No actress worked harder than Eliza, and she appeared constantly as actress, singer, and dancer, playing many roles from her standing repertoire and learning seven new ones, one for each of the seven weeks of the engagement.[30]

It was not easy for her to leave Wignell. She had come to him at a time when her future was very uncertain, and thanks to his personal interest in her, she was now a well-established young actress. During the four seasons she had spent under his management she had learned some forty or more new roles, giving her a repertoire of over seventy parts. She had also developed into an excellent singer and dancer, and would be a valuable actress to any theatrical manager.

At fifteen she had also become very beautiful, and her future must have seemed full of bright prospects indeed when Margaret West offered her an engagement with the Virginia Company, and at last she could look forward to joining Charles that summer in Virginia.

# "The Land of Hog, Hominey, and Hoe-Cake"

BEFORE JOINING CHARLES in Virginia, Eliza had agreed to play in another short summer season at the Southwark Theatre in Philadelphia, again under the management of William Warren, who this time had William Wood as his co-manager. As in the preceding summer, Warren's and Wood's company was made up mostly of actors from the Chestnut Street Theatre.

If she had looked forward to playing as important and challenging roles as she had the preceding summer, she was disappointed. Unfortunately, from the very start, the managers had bad luck. They had to postpone the opening on account of the weather, and at the end of the second week the Philadelphia papers reported the breakout of a fever in the northeastern section of the city. Frightened that it might be the yellow fever, they closed immediately.[1] Any rumor of a yellow fever epidemic would have awakened terrifying thoughts and memories for Eliza.

She left right away for Virginia, where she joined Charles in Alexandria, and very soon after her arrival she married him.[2] She was fifteen.

Alexandria was a thriving shipping and trading center located on the tidewaters of the Potomac across the river from Georgetown and the new federal city of Washington. It was populated for the most part by merchants, craftsmen, and tradesmen, the majority of them Scottish; and the architecture of its buildings showed a more severe and practical taste than the great townhouses Eliza had seen in Philadelphia, New York, and Charleston. Most of the buildings in Alexandria were brick, many of them called "flounder" houses because of their narrow widths, and more often than not, the same compact building served its owner as both shop and living quarters. In keeping with the taste of its thrifty minded populace, Alexandria's chief landmarks—Christ Church, the Presbyterian Meetinghouse, and Gadsby's Tavern—all reflected a simple and neat elegance in their designs. Alexandria's prosperity depended completely on Virginia's plantations and farms, and since its main business was trade, there were fewer slaves there than in any of Virginia's larger towns. When Thomas Wade West had built his theatre, Liberty Hall, in Alexandria his potential audience in this seaport town was the second largest in the state.[3]

It was at Liberty Hall that Eliza and Charles were engaged to play for six weeks beginning in early August 1802. This theatre was on Cameron Street opposite Gadsby's Tavern. It was an attractive house decorated with handsome pediments and deep cornices. The window frames, trusses, and rustic work were all of stone, and there were pedestals on the north front designed for a statue of Shakespeare with the tragic and comic muses at the west and east corners. The location was excellent, and like many other buildings in Alexandria, its design was practical. There were shops on the ground floor, and the theatre (which seated eight hundred), its storage space, and dressing rooms occupied the second and third floors.[4] Liberty Hall was only three years old when Eliza began rehearsals there. It was the newest theatre in Virginia, but it held a sad memory for the actors of the Virginia Company, for in a tragic accident Thomas Wade West had been killed in a fall there the first summer it had opened.[5]

When Eliza had last played with the Virginia Company in Richmond, West had still been alive. Now, since his death, the responsibility of managing the company had been in the hands of his widow, Margaret West. Mrs. West was not the skillful manager her husband had been, and she often shared some of this responsibility with other actors. The season in which Eliza and Charles were to appear in Alexandria was a joint venture of Mrs. West's with John Bernard of the Philadelphia Company.[6]

Together Mrs. West and Bernard had assembled an excellent and versatile company headed by Thomas Cooper and Anne West. The other actors were either from the Philadelphia or the Virginia companies, and Eliza knew almost all of them. Besides Cooper, Bernard, and Anne West, there were William Francis (Wignell's choreographer), Luke Usher, and Matthew Sully, Jr., as well as William Green and his wife, Hope Green. Eliza was working for a new management but not with unfamiliar actors. One of the actresses she did meet for the first time in the company at Alexandria, however, was the extraordinary Susanna Rowson. Mrs. Rowson was very well known to the American public of Eliza's day as an actress and an author. She had written several successful plays, but her best known work was her enormously popular novel, *Charlotte Temple.*

The theatre community in which Eliza and Charles lived and worked was a small, closely knit world. Most of the actors knew each other, sometimes very well, and they often worked together. This meant that within a very short time a company of actors, like the one which Eliza and Charles had joined in Alexandria, could assemble and put together a repertory of extraordinary range. This is precisely what happened that summer. When the season at Liberty Hall opened on 2 August, Margaret West and John Bernard produced a six-week repertory that included poetic tragedy, romantic melodrama, comic opera, farce, ballet, and pantomime.

Eliza and Charles both appeared regularly, Eliza as actress, singer, and dancer. She is not billed for any new parts in the records that survive, but she was especially busy as a dancer, for with William Francis in the company pantomimes appeared frequently on the bill. Eliza not only appeared in the pantomimes, but at various times during the season she was a featured dancer in a minuet and a gavotte, which are both slow and stately dances. She was also featured in a triple hornpipe, a much livelier dance generally done in a sailor costume and always accompanied by hornpipes. In this she probably performed as a soloist. Twice she appeared as Francis's partner, and on the next to last night Alexandria audiences had the opportunity of seeing her dance a Spanish fandango in the second act of *The Mountaineers* with Matthew Sully and Susanna Rowson. This dance usually included some strains sung by the dancers, and it would have been performed with castanets.

After the season closed at Liberty Hall, Eliza took part in a concert held in the elegant ballroom of Gadsby's Tavern.[7] As one of her solos she sang a popular comic song, "The Day of Marriage," for an audience at least a part of which must have known that she and Charles were newlyweds. Directly after her concert she and Charles both made the short trip south by Mount Vernon and across the Rappahannock River to Fredericksburg, where they were to play another engagement.

Like Alexandria, Fredericksburg was also a trading and shipping port. It was located below the falls of the Rappahannock and depended for its trade upon the up-country planters and farmers whose huge wagons of grain, produce, and tobacco always crowded the Fredericksburg streets and wagon yards, awaiting shipment down river to the Potomac and out to sea. Fredericksburg also had a new theatre, located on the southeast corner of Willlam and Prince Edward Streets. It too had been built by Thomas Wade West and was only two years older than Liberty Hall.[8] Eliza and Charles were to play in this theatre with the same company they had appeared with in Alexandria. It was to be a shorter engagement, for Fredericksburg was a smaller town than Alexandria, though the potential audience there expanded with the constant stream of transients moving in and out of town.

Fredericksburg had been named for Frederick, the Prince of Wales, son of George II of England, and its streets bore the names of members of the royal family—Prince Edward, Princess Elizabeth, Princess Anne—but to Americans of Eliza's day Fredericksburg was inseparably connected with George Washington, who had lived there as a boy and whose mother's and sister's home it was. Like Boston, Fredericksburg would have had a distinctively and comfortably English flavor for Eliza, not only in the names of the streets but also in the manners of its people, for the manners of Virginians, especially those of the planters, were often described by her contemporaries as English.[9]

In returning to the South, Eliza was entering once more a very different world from the one in which she had lived and worked in Philadelphia. In the "land of hog, hominey, and hoe-cake"[10]—as William Dunlap once described Virginia—life was slower, more relaxed, and it moved at a "planter's pace."

Though Virginia was the most populous state in the union, numbering nearly a million inhabitants, its agrarian economy made for a widespread population, and there were no large cities with the kind of cosmopolitan audiences for which Eliza had played in New York, Philadelphia, or Charleston. The audiences that came to the Fredericksburg Theatre were nonetheless part of an eager public that had always welcomed actors. Not only did most Virginians appear more interested in plays than churches (as Noah Webster once grumbled),[11] but the lives that many of them led as planters and farmers were isolated and lonely, and they were keenly interested in strangers or travelers. Actors, who traveled a great deal and brought first-hand accounts of life elsewhere, must have been especially attractive to them. It was a congenial and friendly world to which Eliza was returning after living in the more pressured urban atmosphere of Philadelphia.[12]

Immediately after arriving in Fredericksburg, she and Charles went right to work. Opening night was 18 September, only two nights after she had sung in the concert in Alexandria. There were very few new plays to rehearse, and for the most part the company's repertory remained as it had been in Alexandria, with Eliza and Charles playing the same roles. The season lasted a little over a month.[13]

With the closing of the Fredericksburg season, the Bernard-West management ended, and the company disbanded. Eliza said goodbye to Bernard, Francis, and the other actors of the Philadelphia company with whom she had lived and worked so closely for the last four years. They were her last personal contact with Wignell's company. She and Charles then traveled south to Petersburg to begin their life together as members of the Virginia Company.

# "A Theatrical Fracas"

THE STAGE ROAD south to Richmond and Petersburg went through Bowling Green and Hanover. Eliza and Charles were probably traveling with some of the actors with whom they had played in Fredericksburg, and there were small towns along the way where they could have attracted an audience with a play or a concert in a tavern or ordinary, as taverns were called in Virginia. If they did, it would only have been for a night or two, because their eventual destination was Petersburg, where they were to join the rest of Margaret West's company.

Travel overland by stage meant long and exhausting days of bumpy roads, beginning at daybreak and ending at nightfall in a tavern along the way where a young married couple would have been lucky to have had any privacy at all. Stage passengers usually had almost no choice as to where they would stay overnight at those taverns where the stage did stop, and private rooms were always the first taken. Sometimes, if they were lucky, travelers through Virginia would be taken in by planters and treated to sumptuous hospitality. The lonely plantation owners were accustomed to invite complete strangers into their homes, often sending their servants to extend an invitation to them in a tavern or from the road itself. To actors traveling to fulfill an engagement, this could mean an unexpected delay; the lonely host would sometimes press his guests to stay, and the comforts of a plantation mansion were hard to refuse.

It was sometime in early November of 1802 that Eliza and Charles reached Petersburg. It was a small town with a population of slightly less than four thousand, a goodly number of which were slaves. Like Fredericksburg, there was a large transient population. Not only was Petersburg a shipping port, but it was also an important center for horse races. The races were as fashionable as they were popular, ending always with the Race Ball, and during the racing seasons in the fall and spring the town took on the festive air of a carnival. People poured in from miles around. The Virginia Company was well established there, playing at the Back Street Theatre[1] during both the fall and spring racing seasons.

As she began rehearsals for her first season in Petersburg,[2] Eliza was working with the actors who formed the nucleus of Margaret West's Virginia Company, and in finding a place for herself in this company's repertory, she had to begin learning a number of new parts right away. Among them was the role of Zelina in the premiere of a new play *Oberon, or the Siege of Mexico.*

This production must have created a great deal of interest with audiences at the Back Street Theatre, because the playwright, John Daly Burk, lived in Petersburg. Burk was also the author of *The Battle of Bunker Hill* (in the second production of which Eliza, as a child, had made a brief appearance at the John Street Theatre in New York). Although he was best known as a playwright, Burk was a true man of his time, and he had earned a reputation as historian, editor, poet, lawyer, and orator. An Irish political refugee, he had escaped from Ireland to Boston, where he had published a newspaper, become interested in the theatre, and had eventually enjoyed the great popular success of *The Battle of Bunker Hill,* his first of at least eight plays.[3]

As the first performance for *Oberon* approached, rehearsals at the Back Street Theatre must have become hectic, because on the opening night many of the actors were shaky on their lines. This unfortunately often happened at the time, because acting companies had to maintain large repertories, and new plays were inevitably underrehearsed. According to the reviewer writing for the *Petersburg Republican and Advertiser,* there were also other problems.

> The opening of the play with the introduction of a drummer and trum-peter, in a contest of lungs against arms, is a new thought; had these gentlemen left their instruments behind the scenes, they would have appeared to more advantage. . . . The earthquake or temple scene might have had a good effect if any thing like a storm had been exhibited; but as it was the audience would not have known what it was intended for, had not the mother of Oberon been kind enough to give a description of it to her son.
>
> . . . . . . . . . . . . . . . . . . . . . . . .
>
> After saying thus far of what we suppose to be blemishes of this peice, we feel a pleasure in acknowledging, that many of the scenes are strongly delineated . . . the last of these scenes had a powerful effect on the sympathetic feelings of the audience.
>
> Throughout the serious scenes, there is a pathos in the sentiment, and richness in the language, which attracted our admiration; and in many of the comic scenes a fund of humor which kept the audience in bursts of laughter.[4]

Eliza and Charles seem to have been in good form, at least according to this reviewer, who had special praise for both of them. "The pleasing manner in which Mrs. Hopkins performed the part and sung the songs of Zelina had a very good effect," he wrote, and though he felt that one of the two parts that Charles was playing was not well written, "Mr. Hopkins's performance of Ratta and Caustic, were in the best style of acting." In the reviewer's opinion the acting was far superior to the physical production. Eliza was beginning to discover that this was a situation that had existed in the Virginia Company ever since Thomas Wade West's death. Despite the shortcomings of the first night, however, *Oberon* was well received by the public, and the second performance, which took place on the closing night of the season, played to an overflowing house.

After closing in Petersburg, the company traveled north toward Richmond. The country through which they passed was flat and almost barren of any crops with only here and there a field of wheat or Indian corn. Eliza had last traveled this bleak stretch of almost uninterrupted wilderness leading to Manchester and the James River with her stepfather. That had been only four years earlier, shortly after her mother's death. It had been a time of terrible uncertainties for her then, but now she was coming back in far different circumstances. She and Charles were beginning a new life together.

Though Richmond had increased in importance and in population, it had changed little in appearance since Eliza had last seen it. The stage still approached the city from the south across the shallow and rocky James River by means of Mayo's Bridge, and the most conspicuous landmark was the Capitol building on Shockhoe Hill. It towered over the other buildings, and since most of these buildings were obscured by trees, the Capitol looked very much like a Roman temple surrounded by woods, because Thomas Jefferson had designed it along strictly classical lines. The steeple of St. John's Church, already famous for Patrick Henry's oration there, could be seen to the east on Church Hill, but it was not nearly so striking a sight as the Capitol.[5]

Eliza could not but have been struck by the vast contrast between Richmond and Philadelphia, where she had spent the last four seasons. Although Richmond had been the state capital for over twenty years and was the second largest city in Virginia, it was still a small town compared to Philadelphia. Its population was less than six thousand. The hills and ravines on which it had been laid out gave it an untamed and broken appearance. Even the Capitol was rudely enclosed, and the mud was sometimes ankle deep in the unpaved streets.

If Eliza had not played there four years earlier, she would have found the temporary Richmond theatre a great disappointment. It was a makeshift affair located in the Market Hall on 17th Street around the corner from the Bell Tavern and not far from the Capitol. The Virginia Company had been forced to make this temporary location its winter headquarters ever since the old Academy Theatre had burned in 1798.

The opening night in Richmond was on 14 December. Unfortunately, very few records of this season exist.[6] Only four advertisements appear in the Richmond papers from that winter, but this does not mean that the company would not have been playing regularly. Often announcement of the plays was not made in the newspapers but on handbills, and sometimes the bill for the next performance night might even be announced at the theatre after the final curtain. Judging by the parts she had already played in Virginia, Eliza probably appeared regularly that winter in Richmond. Of the four advertisements that do exist, three of them include plays with parts from her repertoire.

It would have been during this Richmond engagement that Eliza received word that Thomas Wignell had died from an infection received in a bleeding treatment. Wignell's death was a great loss to the entire theatrical community, for there was hardly an important actor in the country whom his career had not touched. He had certainly been a strong influence in both Charles's and Eliza's careers, and he had taken a personal interest in Eliza at a time when she had especially needed his help and guidance. Wignell's untimely and sudden death had come only a month after his marriage to Ann Merry.

The winter season at the Richmond Market Hall ended with the welcome announcement to the public that subscription had begun for a new brick theatre to be built on the site of the old Academy Theatre on Shockhoe Hill.

Norfolk was the next stand on the Virginia Company's circuit, and Eliza was scheduled to make her debut there in March of 1803. This was an important debut. Her success with the Norfolk public would strongly affect her future with the Virginia Company, because Norfolk was the largest city in Virginia and the base of operations for the Virginia Company, which played a long spring and summer season there every year. The Wests made their home in Norfolk, and the Fenchurch Street Theatre, a handsome brick building on Fenchurch Street between Main and Bermuda, was the first theatre that Thomas Wade West had built in Virginia.[7]

Winning a following with the Norfolk public was not easy. Audiences there were of a decidedly different cast from the social set that attended the theatre at Petersburg or the up-country planters, farmers, and Scottish merchants that composed the bulk of the audiences in Alexandria, Fredericksburg, or Richmond. Norfolk was a seaport. Its population included many English merchants and a French community as well as shipbuilders, sea captains, and sailors.[8] The public there was probably the most cosmopolitan audience for which the Virginia Company played, but it could be unpredictable, tough, and rowdy.

Margaret West scheduled Eliza's debut for the opening night of the season and chose to introduce her to the Norfolk audiences as a dramatic actress rather than as a comedienne. This was a definite change for Eliza, who at this time of her career was making the difficult transition from child actress to ingenue and young leading lady. Both of the parts Mrs. West cast her in for the Norfolk opening were leading roles (sentimental heroines, her contemporaries would have called them), Louisa in August von Kotzebue's *Sighs* and Rosina in William Shield's comic opera *Rosina,* and they were new to her repertoire. Louisa is a difficult part, and it is filled with the kind of sense and sentiment that early nineteenth-century audiences loved, Louisa's big scene coming in a tearful reunion with her father. Kotzebue called *Sighs* a comedy, but we would think of it today as a melodrama. *Rosina,* which was always played as an afterpiece or farce, is a comic opera, and its heroine is a classic example in the line of heroines that appear throughout eighteenth-century English sentimental comedies and comic operas. She is a lady of impeccable birth, character, and virtue who is left as a child in the care of a rustic family and must labor in the fields as a reaper. Her great beauty attracts the lord of the manor, but it is not until her stepmother reveals she is well born that she agrees to marry him. During the course of the play Rosina's virtue is assaulted by the squire's older brother, who attempts unsuccessfully to abduct her. The setting and songs reflect a bucolic and romantic feeling, and in style it is typical of the English comic operas in which Eliza often played.

So it was as a dramatic actress that Eliza made her debut for the Norfolk public. She was billed as "late Miss Arnold of the Philadelphia Theatre," and a reviewer for the *Norfolk Herald* described her performance.

> Mrs. Hopkins' figure and countenance are pretty, and we believe she endeavoured to deserve applause; being her first appearance at this theatre, she appeared at the commencement of the play, much abashed . . . however, toward the conclusion, she seemed at home and gave general satisfaction, particularly in the farce, in which she sang with great taste and judgement; she is somewhat defective in action and has but a weak voice. Time and practice may procure her the one and strengthen the other.[9]

Playing the new parts must have robbed Eliza of some authority, and her nervousness and lack of experience as a dramatic actress evidently showed in her performance. But there were other reasons for her to feel shaky.

Margaret West, unlike her husband, was careless about technical matters. From the many theatrical correspondants in the Virginia papers (in Eliza's day the forerunners of the critics) one reads of open windows in Mrs. West's theatres without shutters or sash, of musicians playing "Yankee Doodle" between the acts of a tragedy, and of "damn your eyes" and "blood of a bitch" being audible from behind the closed curtain during a scenery shift.[10] In an embarrassing incident two years before Eliza played her debut at the Fenchurch Street Theatre, a correspondant reported that "owing to the ponderosity of Mrs. Rowson, the springs of a trap door gave way, and not only the leading lady disappeared, but she carried little Mrs. Stuart down also."[11] However much the sailors in the pit and gallery enjoyed this kind of mishap, such carelessness could hardly have made Mrs. West's actors feel secure. This was especially true for Eliza, who had been accustomed to the superb technical crew of the Chestnut Street Theatre, where such technical problems did not exist.

After her debut Eliza appeared as a comedienne in a line of parts both old and new to her. In the week following the Easter layoff she played Moggy McGilpin in *The Highland Reel*, and Matthew Sully, whom she had known since she was a child, was Shelty, her leading man. Though both reviewers for the *Herald* liked his and Eliza's performance, they were disappointed in the rest of the company and with the production as a whole. One of them frankly asked why Anne West was not playing Moggy.

The reviewers for the *Herald*, however, were not the only critics of the performance that night. Audiences at the Fenchurch Street Theatre—which sometimes included well-known prostitutes from "the purlieus of Water Street, Bank Street, and Lee's Wharf"[12]—were not hampered by any misplaced sense of propriety. During the afterpiece, a member of the gallery, displeased with what he saw on the stage, loudly voiced his disapproval. When one of the actors stepped to the edge of the stage and commanded him to be silent, the irate galleryite, having paid the price of admission and no doubt feeling he was not getting his money's worth, managed to create such a disturbance that he was eventually "seized by the doorkeepers, and kicked downstairs." There he was collared by one of the actors in the company who proceeded to slug it out with him in the alley.[13] In describing this incident the *Herald* admonished Mrs. West to look to her actors and discreetly warned that "a theatrical fracas soon gets abroad and is seldom reported with any reputation to the parties." Reputations aside, the Norfolk engagement had thus far been rough going.[14]

Eliza and Charles must have been relieved to suspend the season in Norfolk in the middle of May and travel the one hundred and fifty miles back up the James River to the friendlier environment of Petersburg to play a short engagement at the Back Street Theatre during the spring races.[15] It was a shorter season than they had played there the preceding fall, and since there were few new plays to rehearse, it was also a less hectic one. But they had hardly opened in Petersburg before it was time to travel back down the James again in early June to play at the Fenchurch Street Theatre through the summer and try once again to capture the fancy of the erratic and unpredictable Norfolk public.

There was more for Eliza to face during a summer season in Norfolk than a tough public, however. Summers in that part of Virginia were suffocatingly hot, though the weather was often variable, and easterly winds could suddenly bring a nor'easter with three days or so of quite cold weather. Conditions in Norfolk were made no pleasanter, or healthier, by the presence of open sewage ditches, dusty unpaved streets, and swarms of mosquitos bred in the waters that almost surrounded the little seaport. The town itself was quite spread out. A contemporary drawing of Norfolk shows the steeples of its mostly wooden buildings almost perfectly balanced by the many masts of ships at anchor along the wharves that lined the banks of the Elizabeth River. Like in Boston and in Fredericksburg, a strong English flavor prevailed in the taste for luxury items and furnishings in the taverns or boardinghouses where Eliza and Charles lodged.

As the summer season moved along at the Fenchurch Street Theatre, the reviews in the *Norfolk Herald,* the only Norfolk paper at that time, became more favorable, especially after John Bernard and William Green joined the company. With these two new leading men the company could offer the public almost a completely different repertory from what it had in the spring. For the actors that meant constant rehearsal.

Eliza and Charles had their benefit on 1 July, and when the Norfolk season closed on 13 July,[16] Eliza had completed her first full swing through the Virginia Company's circuit. There had been little or no time for her and Charles to settle down, because the company had been almost constantly on the move. From a professional point of view the technical problems under Margaret West's management had undoubtedly often been a nuisance, but Eliza had made important gains with this management, because she had begun to play far more challenging roles than she had in Philadelphia. More important still, she was with Charles.

# David Poe

FOLLOWING THE NORFOLK SEASON Eliza and Charles traveled back to Richmond, where they both appeared in a concert at the assembly room of the Bell Tavern,[1] and a week after this concert they were back in Alexandria ready to begin Eliza's second tour of the Virginia circuit.[2] It was August 1803.

They both attracted important attention in the Alexandria papers during this season at Liberty Hall. A reviewer for the *Alexandria Times and District of Columbia Daily Advertiser* marveled at Charles's skillful portrayal of old men: "To see a very youth hit off the manners of old age so successfully is a sort of theatrical phenomenon."[3] Eliza, who was already beginning to gain some notoriety with the Virginia public, had one of the best notices of her entire career with the Virginia Company in this same paper.

> Mrs. Hopkins . . . is amply compensated by the loud plaudits with which she is always received, which evince, that of all the ladies of the theatre, she is at least a second favorite with the public—though perhaps incapable of ever arriving at the eminence of a Siddons or a Merry. Mrs. Hopkins' interesting figure, her *correct* performance, and the accuracy with which she always commits her part, together with her sweetly melodious voice when she charms us with a song, have deservedly raised her to that respectable rank which she indisputably holds in the public favor.[4]

The usual fall engagements in Fredericksburg[5] and Petersburg[6] followed, but there are very few records to tell precisely what or how frequently Eliza played in either of these short seasons. This is unfortunate, for it would be interesting to know how Hope Green's presence in the company affected Eliza's casting. Mrs. Green had returned to the Virginia Company with her husband William Green during the Norfolk season, and she had appeared regularly since then. Both she and Eliza played many of the same roles, and their assignments would have inevitably overlapped. Of those records which do survive from this period, however, one is an ad in Petersburg for Eliza and Charles's benefit[7] on Saturday, 12 November 1803. This is the first record of Eliza's appearance in Richard Brinsley Sheridan's great eighteenth-century comedy *The School for Scandal*. As the Virginia Company's leading lady, Anne West played Lady Teazle. Charles played two parts, Crabtree and Moses; and Eliza was cast in the role of Maria. Since it was the Hopkinses' benefit, they both sang between the play and the afterpiece, and Eliza also appeared in a solo dance.

It was just after Christmas when the actors arrived back in Richmond for the winter season.[8] The new theatre there was still unfinished, and Mrs. West, with William Green now acting as her co-manager, moved her company into another temporary theatre in Quarrier's Coach Shop on the corner of Cary and Seventh Street. This new location was below the capitol and west of the Market Hall. The season opened on 21 December. Business was good, and regular performances continued through the holidays and into January and February, Eliza and Charles both appearing often, for the most part in plays already in the company's repertory.

Just as benefits were about to begin, news reached Richmond of a devastating fire in Norfolk, and details of this disaster quickly became known. On 22 February, a cold, drifty, snowy night, a fire had broken out in Norfolk in the area south of Main Street near Market Square. It was believed to have been started by an overturned candle in a wine cellar. Huge flames quickly spread over that part of the city below Main Street, eventually reaching the docks, where many of the ships at anchor also caught fire and drifted into the harbor, flames engulfing their masts, sails, and rigging. An inferno raged for nearly seven hours. When the final blazes had been extinguished, the bewildered citizens of Norfolk found that some three hundred buildings were in ruins, many of them having been deliberately blown to bits by explosives in attempts to halt the fire. There were scores of deaths and injuries.[9]

Like their fellow actors, Eliza and Charles would have been greatly relieved to hear that the flames had not reached north to Fenchurch Street and that the theatre was not damaged. Margaret West's home on Main Street around the corner from the theatre was also safe. The actors immediately announced a benefit for the fire sufferers, and playing one of the season's biggest successes, *John Bull,* they turned over receipts of $230 to the stricken Norfolk citizens.

When news of the fire reached Richmond, the season at Quarrier's temporary theatre was already in its closing weeks, and Royall Tyler's comedy *The Contrast* was chosen for one of the actor's benefit nights. This was Eliza's first acquaintance with this play, which after nearly twenty years of popularity, was still a good attraction: "The first essay of American genius in the dramatic art,"[10] the Virginia Company's advertisement announced. There is no cast list to tell whether Eliza actually appeared in the play, but she would have been right for any of the four women's parts.

After a short layoff for the Easter holidays the Richmond season closed in early April, ending an engagement of sixteen weeks.

It was impossible to play the spring and summer seasons in Norfolk. A great portion of the city was in ruins, and its public was in no mood for theatregoing. This meant that the company would lose crucial playing weeks, because the success of its circuit depended a great deal on the Norfolk engagement. Rather than cease their operations until the fall stand in Alexandria, however, Mrs. West and William Green decided to extend their usual short season in Petersburg[11] during the spring races and then return the company to the temporary theatre in Richmond for the summer. In this way they would keep the actors employed and avoid the risk of losing them by disbanding the company until the fall. In order to attract audiences for the added weeks in Petersburg they produced a number of new plays, one of them a new comedy by Charleston playwright James Workman called *Liberty in Louisiana,* which had just had its premiere performance in Charleston. At the end of the extended stand in Petersburg, Eliza and Charles, who were by now well known to audiences at the Back Street Theatre, presented a concert there under their own management.[12]

The following week they were back with the company in Richmond again, ready to begin the summer season at Quarrier's temporary theatre as Mrs. West and William Green had planned.[13] The opening play was Thomas Morton's comedy *Speed the Plow.* Eliza and Charles were both cast in important roles— Eliza as the ingenue Susan Ashfield and Charles as Sir Abel Handy, one of the character parts.

As Henry, the hero around whose identity the plot centers, the managers cast a young actor named David Poe, who had just joined the company and who was making his Richmond debut. Though this would probably have been the first time that either Eliza or Charles had met him, David had had the opportunity of seeing them both at the Holliday Street Theatre in Baltimore, where his family lived and where before becoming an actor, he had been an avid theatregoer.

— David Poe had only recently finished playing his first professional engagement. He was the 19-year-old son of the Irish-born American patriot Major David Poe, Sr., a Revolutionary War figure, friend of the marquis de Lafayette, and sometimes called "General Poe" by the Baltimore citizens who remembered his services to that city during the war. David had been apprenticed to the law by his father, but he had ambitions of becoming an actor, and in spite of his father's disapproval he had given up his law studies, left Baltimore, and obtained an engagement with Alexandre Placide's company at the Charleston Theatre in December of 1803.

His first professional season in Charleston had been difficult. He was an American with virtually no experience except as an amateur in Baltimore, and he had been in a company of actors most of whom had excellent English or European training and considerable professional reputations. He had had no repertoire, except what little he might have learned as an amateur, and in the five-month season he had played with Placide's company he had been assigned over twenty roles to prepare and perform. At that time actors did not begin their careers playing only in small parts, and some of the roles he had been assigned were substantial ones. He had felt the pressure of this work very keenly, and it had showed in his performances in Charleston. The reviewers had written of his diffidence, his timidity, and the paralyzing stage fright that had made him rush his speeches and cause himself embarrasing memory slips. It had been the beginning of a tough apprenticeship, but David had important assets for an actor. He was good looking, he had a fine voice, and he had a flair for speaking poetry well. His natural talents were combined with a nervous and highly strung sensitivity, also an important asset for an actor.[14]

David worked very closely with Eliza and Charles that summer at the temporary theatre in Richmond, and it was a very important time for all three of them, especially Charles, because two weeks after the opening he had the opportunity to make his first attempt at management.

When Mrs. West and William Green decided to withdraw as managers of the summer season in Richmond, Charles, in a partnership that included two other actors in the company, became one of the co-managers. This meant that not only did he have some say in the choice of the repertory, but, far more important, he had some control over his own and Eliza's assignments as well. It also meant that he was investing his own money in the expenses of the house and sharing whatever risk there was of the season's ending in a loss.

The first play chosen under this new management was George Colman II's popular comedy The Heir at Law, a play that would still be popular in America nearly one hundred years later when the great Joseph Jefferson used it as a vehicle. In Eliza's day, however, The Heir at Law was a comparatively new play. Eliza played Caroline Dormer, the heroine, and David Poe was her lover Henry Morland. Charles was Dr. Pangloss, the demure tutor just awarded the "degree of A double S" and full of classical misquotations. Eliza's part abounded with the sentiment of what actors of a later generation would call the Old Comedy, or (perhaps more properly) sentimental comedy. These plays are filled with Caroline Dormers, virtuous, faithful, and full of moral sentiment and impeccable prose. Considering the taste for satire in the period, it is easy to believe that they were sometimes conceived as burlesque. Eliza played her share of these young women. It was an important line of parts for her.

Now that Charles was in a position to influence her casting, Eliza, who during her entire association with the Virginia Company seems to have been determined to stretch her range beyond the comic operas and sentimental comedies in which she had so often appeared in Philadelphia, played Stella in James Boaden's play The Maid of Bristol. At this time of her career the vivaciousness of Moggy McGilpin or the predictability of Caroline Dormer were far less challenging than portraying the bitterness and despair of this leading character. It was a difficult role with long speeches and scenes of sustained tension that demanded far more of Eliza's instrument than almost anything she had yet played. Both Charles and David were in the play with her. David was again her lover and leading man, and Charles played Dr. Cranium, a quack phrenologist.

The engagement at the temporary theatre in Richmond closed on 1 September. It had been a very valuable time for all three of these young actors, and the work they did during those seven summer weeks is extraordinary when one considers that both Eliza and David were not yet twenty, and Charles could hardly have been much older.

# Replacing Anne West

IN EARLY SEPTEMBER Eliza, Charles, and David all began another season under Mrs. West's management; and since she no longer planned to keep Alexandria on her circuit, they traveled straight to Fredericksburg, where they played for five weeks.[1] By mid-October they had returned to Petersburg for the customary fall season during the races.[2]

The Back Street Theatre was crowded on the opening night. Mrs. West had chosen to begin the season with Adam Cherry's comedy *The Soldier's Daughter*, a play that was new to the repertory. Anne West was in the leading role of the Widow Cheerly, and Eliza, Charles, and David were all in good featured parts. The performance was an enormous success, and a glowing notice appeared in the next issue of *The Intelligencer*, praising Anne West, Eliza, Charles, and David Poe as well, who the reviewer felt had given an excellent performance and showed great potential for becoming a valuable member of the Virginia Company. Though the play was a comedy, Eliza, continuing to add more serious parts to her repertoire, played Mrs. Malfort, a highly dramatic role. In writing of her work, the reviewer for the *Intelligencer* spoke of her in the same breath with the company's leading actress: "Among those who acquitted themselves with the greatest eclat, I cannot omit to mention the names of Mrs. West, Jr., in the character of the Widow Cheerly and Mrs. Hopkins in Mrs. Malfort—the sprightly vitality of the one, and the placid melancholy of the other, alternately awakened the opposite feelings of innocent hilarity, and heart-rending sorrow."[3]

Soon after the opening the company began rehearsals for *Bethlem Gabor*, the second of John Daly Burk's plays to be produced in Petersburg by Mrs. West since Eliza had joined her company, but the excitement surrounding the production of this wildly romantic melodrama was soon eclipsed in the public mind by an event of far more stirring interest. Aaron Burr had arrived in Petersburg.

It was barely three months after his fatal duel with Alexander Hamilton, and Burr was under indictment for murder in New Jersey and New York. He had fled into the South immediately after the duel and was now traveling through Petersburg on his way back to Washington, for he was still serving the final year of his term as vice-president. He was received with great hospitality in Petersburg, and the festivities in his honor were elaborate. On Tuesday, 30 October, he was entertained at a public dinner and then escorted to the Back Street Theatre, where the Virginia Company played a performance of its new success, *The Soldier's Daughter,* with Eliza, Charles, and David all in the company. When Burr was introduced in the theatre that night he received a standing ovation. His visit was the highlight of the Petersburg season.[4]

The new theatre in Richmond was still under construction and would not be ready for another year yet, so it was necessary for the company to spend its winter season once more at Quarrier's temporary theatre.[5] Inadequate as this improvised theatre was, the managers must have expected to fill it regularly, because they scheduled an extra performance during the week and played on Monday, Wednesday, Friday, and Saturday nights. Richmond was beginning to become as important to the Virginia Company's circuit as Norfolk.

Not long into this season Anne West became very ill, and the managers announced that Eliza would replace her as Mary Thornberry in *John Bull* and Emily Worthington in *The Poor Gentleman.* That the management should cast Eliza in these important parts speaks very highly of the standing she now had in the Virginia Company. These roles require a leading lady, and few actresses of her age—she was eighteen—would have had the maturity or skill to play them. It was a difficult assignment and a good deal of hard work, and as replacement under such circumstances inevitably is, it probably had to be done under great pressure within a very short time.

The technical situation must have been improving with William Green now involved in the management, because during the Christmas holidays the company presented a very successful production of a new comic pantomime, *Christmas Gambols or Winter's Amusements,* that included "an exact representation of a sleighing match and a snow storm."[6] Eliza, David, and Charles all danced in this entertainment, Eliza and David performing a strathspey, a slow Scottish dance, while Charles did a mock minuet, probably a comic version of a minuet. Eliza and David appeared together very frequently that season.

Eliza and Charles were both steadily becoming important actors in the Virginia Company, and when benefits began after the holidays, they were each given separate nights.

Shortly after Eliza's benefit the weather turned bitter cold, and piercing winds drove temperature well below freezing.[7] This was unusual for Richmond, and the theatre closed. During this cold wave Anne West died. This was a great loss to the Virginia Company, for she was a brilliant actress. Her death was noted in newspapers all over Virginia, and her obituary in Petersburg described her as "the most distinguished ornament of the Virginia stage."[8]

Important changes were to take place in the organization of the Virginia Company after Anne West's death. Most significant of all, her mother, Margaret West, would become much less active in the management, and William Green would begin to assume most of the responsibility. The company's repertory and casting would also be strongly affected. For the time being, however, the casting was advantageous to Eliza, because she had taken over some of the roles Anne West had played. This was valuable experience, but in one sense it was a mixed blessing: it meant that Eliza had to compete in the public's mind with the memory of a popular favorite, and she would have had to work hard to make the roles she had taken over uniquely her own.

It had been over a year since the Virginia Company had played at the Fenchurch Street Theatre in Norfolk, and after the winter season closed in Richmond, William Green moved the company to Norfolk. In planning this important season,[9] he felt the loss of Anne West keenly, but he did have an advantage in that the Norfolk public had seen none of the new productions that the company had added to its repertory during the last year. A number of these plays had proved to be popular successes, and Eliza had excellent parts in them, so that when the season opened in mid-March she was one of the company's leading actresses. This was to be by far the best exposure that she had had in the Virginia Company, because it was not until the final weeks of that Norfolk season that Green hired Mrs. Wilmot[10] to fill the gap left in the company by Anne West's death.

Mrs. Wilmot was a highly respected and well-known actress with nearly twenty years experience—more than twice Eliza's. Her career had begun in London at the Haymarket and Covent Garden Theatres, and she had made her American debut with Wignell, enjoying great success in Philadelphia, Boston, and Charleston (where she had spent the last six seasons). As a child, Eliza had known her very briefly when they were both in Wignell's company in Philadelphia six years earlier. Mrs. Wilmot's presence in the Virginia Company would affect Eliza's assignments, a fact of theatrical life that Eliza undoubtedly realized. The older actress played many of the roles that Eliza had taken over from Anne West, and as the company's new leading lady she would have first refusal over them.

While the Virginia Company was continuing its Norfolk season into the early summer, David Poe had left the company and gone home to Baltimore, where he arranged to make his debut at the Holliday Street Theatre under the management of William Warren and William Wood (who had succeeded Thomas Wignell as managers of the Philadelphia Company).[11] David's debut was set for Friday, 7 June 1805, and it must have been an all important night for him. He had often sat in the audience at the Holliday Street Theatre, had dreamed of becoming an actor there, and now at last he could appear on its stage himself and prove to his father and the rest of his family that he was able to make his way in his chosen profession. David had mostly been successful in poetic plays, and for this debut he played Young Norval, the leading role, in John Home's verse tragedy *Douglas*. If General Poe were in the audience on the night of his son's Baltimore debut, he could have taken some pride in knowing that David was playing with one of the most distinguished actors in the country, because Thomas Cooper was in the part of Glenalvon. Whether or not David's family were impressed with his debut, it is not known; but William Warren and William Wood must have been, because they hired him for their summer season in Alexandria and gave him good assignments.

Meantime, after closing in Norfolk, Eliza and Charles returned to Richmond, where Eliza appeared in a concert at the Eagle Tavern,[12] and a little over a week after this concert she and Charles traveled north to Washington, where for the second time in both their careers they were scheduled to appear together in a new theatre there.

# "An Affectionate Wife"

WHEN THEY CAME TO WASHINGTON in the fall of 1805, Eliza and Charles had been married a little over three years. During that time they had both established excellent professional reputations for themselves. In the five years during which he had been associated with the Virginia Company, Charles's position as an actor had steadily become more and more important. He was a born character actor, and since he was suited to play parts much older than his actual age, he had been able to appear in the rich line of character parts in the plays of Goldsmith, Sheridan, George Colman II, and the English writers of eighteenth-century sentimental comedy. These playwrights, many of them actors, created a gallery of picturesque and salty characters for the light comedian: Dr. Pangloss, Tony Lumpkin, Dr. Ollapod, Sir Peter Teazle, Major Benbow, Sir Abel Handy, Lord Priory. It was in these roles that Charles had learned his craft and built his reputation. Eliza, too, had become an important and well-known actress. Though she was still primarily an ingenue, she had been often cast in leading roles and for a time had even taken over some of the roles that Anne West had played. She was not yet ready to step into a line of parts that required a leading lady, however. At eighteen she lacked the maturity, but for the time being she could still expect her skills as a comedienne, singer, and dancer to be consistently in demand. There would be ample opportunity for her to grow in the Virginia Company, and there was certainly no reason for her or Charles to seek work elsewhere. If they remained, they would eventually be able to make their home in Richmond or Norfolk, and as the Wests and Greens had done, remain active year round on the Virginia circuit. Charles had already had some success as a manager, and with his growing reputation he would be able to make other such ventures; perhaps one day he might even become part of the management of the Virginia Company himself. They were both still very young, and as they began rehearsals in Washington, their future life together must have looked deceptively settled and bright.

It had been five years since Eliza and Charles had played in the first theatrical season in Washington. That had been under Wignell's management at the Lottery Hotel. Now the Virginia Company was scheduled to play in the newly constructed Washington Theatre located on 11th and C Streets (on the opposite side of Pennsylvania Avenue from the present National Theatre). Subscription for this theatre, the first to be built in the five-year-old city, had begun in April 1803. The theatre had opened the following year, but instead of an acting company the first season had featured a variety of entertainments including 3½-feet-high marionettes billed as Mr. Maginnis's "artificial comedians," from London. As members of the first company of genuine comedians in this new theatre, Eliza and Charles were taking part in an important occasion. [1]

As manager, William Green had excellent prospects for a successful season in Washington. The addition of Mrs. Wilmot had strengthened his company considerably, and as a special attraction for the new theatre he had arranged for John Hodgkinson to appear with his company. Hodgkinson was a brilliant actor whom Eliza's contemporaries often compared with Garrick. [2] He was a versatile actor and an excellent singer, and he enjoyed enormous success and popularity. Selfish, demanding, and ruthlessly ambitious, he had come to America after a short career in England and had joined the American Company, becoming in a short time one of its leading performers and eventually rising to the position of co-manager. For the last two years he had been in Charleston, where he had been associated in management with Placide.

For the Washington opening Green chose two comedies, Elizabeth Inchbald's *Wives as They Were and Maids as They Are* and George Colman II's *Ways and Means.* Eliza and Charles both appeared prominently: Charles in the first play as Lord Priory, the leading role, and Eliza, in the second, as Kitty, the ingenue, "young, wild, frank . . . her mind full of fun, her eyes full of fire, her head full of novels, and her heart full of love."[3] Though not enthusiastic about the opening night performance by the company, the reviewer for the *National Intelligencer* was delighted by the new theatre. He reported dutifully, however, that the audience was pleased with the plays even though he was not, and he also grumbled about some trouble with smelly lamps. [4]

Trouble with the lamps was but the first misfortune that was to face the company that season. Hardly had they opened than they received the shocking news that John Hodgkinson, who was to join them the week following the opening, had contracted yellow fever on his way to Washington and had died at a tavern just north of Washington near the small town of Bladensburg, Maryland. [5] This was a severe blow, because Hodgkinson would have been an important addition to the company and a sure draw as well. It also meant that the repertory would have to be changed drastically. Whatever casting difficulties existed as a result of Hodgkinson's death, they were not to Charles Hopkins's disadvantage. When Green announced the Washington premiere of *The School for Scandal,* Charles was cast as Sir Peter Teazle, and he was probably replacing Hodgkinson. Mrs. Wilmot was Lady Teazle, but Eliza did not appear in this production. Though she had played Maria with the Virginia Company, Mrs. Green played the part in the Washington premiere. David Poe, in the meantime, had returned to the company from his engagement in Alexandria, and he was cast in the important role of Joseph Surface. The season continued through September, and benefits for the company's leading actors, of whom Charles Hopkins now numbered, were played the first week in October.[6] Then the theatre closed temporarily and the company moved to Fredericksburg.[7]

Actors lived in dread of the yellow fever, and their constant travel and appearances before the public made the danger of infection an ever present reality to them. In Eliza's day it was not known that mosquitos carried this killer disease, and people believed that the infection was borne in the air itself. Panic always accompanied any news of an individual case or especially an outbreak— panic and usually flight to escape contagion. Hodgkinson's death of the yellow fever in Maryland had cast a pall over the beginning of the Washington season, but fortunately it had not been followed by other cases in the Washington area. There had been scattered reports elsewhere of a "malignant fever,"[8] but no cause for widespread alarm.

Sometime during the short Fredericksburg season or shortly after the company had returned to Washington, Charles fell ill. Perhaps, like Hodgkinson, it was an isolated case of the yellow fever with which he was stricken. If so, Eliza could do little for him but helplessly sit by and watch the dreadful disease at work. It was a grim and fatal ordeal—high fever accompanied by delirium and finally black vomit. Charles died in Washington on Saturday, 26 October. It was early fall, the same time of year Eliza had lost her mother. "He has left," his obituary in the *Richmond Enquirer* read, "an affectionate wife to lament his loss."[9] At eighteen Eliza was a widow.

The Virginia Company was now even more seriously weakened. In the best tradition of their profession, however, the actors reopened the Washington Theatre two days after Charles's death, and a little over a week later Eliza had a benefit.

She chose Matthew G. Lewis's romantic drama, *Adelmorn the Outlaw,* a play she and Charles had often played together, and one in which at different times they had appeared in the same part. Eliza had played the page Herman in Philadelphia; but in the Virginia Company she was cast as Orilla, one of the young heroines, and Charles had played Herman. In the play Herman is in love with Orilla, and they have several scenes and songs together, including one long duet. On this benefit night the following lines from their opening scene must have had a special poignancy for Eliza, for she had often played the scene with Charles.

ORILLA. I must confide to you my dearest, in truth my only secret. Know then, I love—

HERMAN. Me, dear Orilla?

ORILLA. No, indeed, dear Herman; but you will stare when I tell you that the happy man is no other than . . . my husband!

The play appeared often in the Virginia Company's repertory, and it had been one of Eliza's and Charles's popular vehicles.

Winter was coming and despite the bad houses, Green continued the season into December. Stoves were placed in the lobby to make the new theatre more comfortable, and two separate editorials appeared in the *National Intelligencer* asking the public's support for the theatre,[10] but there is no evidence that business improved, and the Virginia Company closed the week before Christmas.

Eliza came back to Richmond alone. Her life now was vastly changed. She had joined the Virginia Company to be with Charles, and the short life she had shared with him in Virginia had brought them very close. Their work had brought them together literally morning, noon, and night. It is likely that during their entire marriage they had never been apart. Charles's death must have been a heartbreaking loss for Eliza. In a short time she would learn to forget, but for now, as she returned to Richmond after Christmas, she faced not only the memories of her life there with Charles, but also her own disturbing and perplexing grief. Fortunately, there was also work.

The season in Richmond began with great excitement, because the new theatre had finally been completed.[11] It had been three years since plans to build this theatre had begun to take shape, and now, at last, the opening was announced for late January. "The theatre, although not completed, already exhibits taste and elegance," the opening announcement in the Richmond *Gazette* read, "and no pains have been omitted in rendering it comfortable for the accommodation of the visitors."[12] The new theatre was of brick and included two tiers of boxes, a pit, offices, dressing rooms, and a green room. It seated about six hundred and was located on Academy Square, the site of the old Academy Theatre.[13]

For this important first season in the new Richmond Theatre, Mrs. West rejoined William Green in the management, and on the opening night the Virginia Company presented Elizabeth Inchbald's comedy *Wives as They Were and Maids as They Are* (the same play with which it had opened the Washington season) and John O'Keeffee's comic opera *The Poor Soldier*. Eliza was featured as Norah, the leading part in the afterpiece, a role that had now been in her repertoire for eight years and one in which she had been very successful.

David Poe had also returned to Richmond with the company, and during this premiere season at the new theatre he was often in the same plays as Eliza. The managers frequently cast them as a couple, as lovers, or young husband and wife, and they worked very closely together. They had also often appeared together the preceding season, so they were already well acquainted. David was very handsome, and though he was nervous, highly strung, and had a volatile temper, there was an appealing sensitivity about him, and Eliza found him very attractive. David was also very strongly attracted to her. Small wonder; she was very beautiful. They were both unattached and still very young—Eliza was nineteen and David two years older—and it was probably not surprising to many who knew them that on 14 March 1806, five months after Charles Hopkins's death,

David Poe executed a marriage bond between himself and "Eliza Hopkins, widow of Charles D. Hopkins."[14]

For her benefit at the end of March Eliza played Lady Randolph in John Home's tragedy *Douglas*. This was her first attempt at playing a tragic heroine, and it was in a demanding part, for Lady Randolph was considered one of the great parts and a real test of the fine actress. Both Mrs. Siddons and Mrs. Whitlock had had great success in this character, and Richmond audiences had seen Mrs. West as Lady Randolph earlier that season. Eliza's first introduction to this role had been when her mother had played it in the Assembly Room in Portsmouth, New Hampshire, the first year she had come to America. That had been nine long years ago, another lifetime it must have seemed to Eliza. The production of *Douglas* at the Richmond Theatre was an unusual one, because Mrs. Wilmot played the young hero, Norval, and she was one of the few actresses ever to attempt this part in America.

Eliza's benefit night was the last time that she was billed as Mrs. Hopkins. The theatre closed during Holy Week, and when it reopened after Easter to continue the season into May, she and David were married.

# "Her Best and Most Sympathetic Friends"

IT WAS TIME for a change. Eliza and David needed a fresh start in different surroundings, and during the spring of 1806 they began making plans to leave Virginia.

It was most likely through John Bernard, who had often worked with Eliza, knew her, and admired her, that she and David were both able to secure engagements with a new management that Bernard had formed that spring in partnership with James Dickenson and Snelling Powell in Boston. Their engagement was to begin at the Federal Street Theatre in the fall.

Meantime, they had three months to fill, and they were not idle. After the season in Richmond closed in the early part of the summer, Eliza put her life with the Virginia Company behind her, and she and David traveled north to Philadelphia, where they had four weeks work at the Chestnut Street Theatre.[1] Although they had both worked for the Warren and Wood management before, David had never played in Philadelphia, so he made his debut there in late June as Young Norval in *Douglas,* a role that was becoming an important part for him. In the afterpiece on the same night Eliza played Rosina. The ad announcing these plays reminded the public that Mrs. Poe was the former Miss Arnold, whom Philadelphia audiences should remember and who was making "her first appearance on this stage these five years."[2] Philadelphians had never known her as Mrs. Hopkins.

For Eliza returning to the Chestnut Street Theatre was like coming back to her first home, but she found the company considerably changed since she had left. Most conspicuous of all was the absence of Thomas Wignell, whose jaunty figure with his inveterate cane and cocked hat was no longer seen on Chestnut Street. In the constant shift of personnel that always occurred in acting companies of that time many of Eliza's friends had gone on to other parts of the country, but William Francis, the choreographer with whom she had worked so closely, was still there, as were both William Warren and William Wood, who were now the managers. The most important new personage in the company was Joseph Jefferson I, the grandfather of Joseph Jefferson of Rip Van Winkle fame. Jefferson was a prototype of the superb performer that the early nineteenth-century repertory system produced: basically a character actor and at home in any style play. Both Eliza and David appeared with him that summer, Eliza for the first and only time of her career.

Traveling further north, they managed to land a short engagement during July in New York, where they played in Joseph Delacroix's newly constructed outdoor theatre in Vauxhall Garden. This "elegant place of public amusement,"[3] as a contemporary described it, was located next to the present Public Theatre at Astor Place, at that time a considerable distance from the center of town. Vauxhall Garden was only a year old, but already it was very popular and fashionable, and every evening crowds of New Yorkers took the carriages that ran from St. Paul's Chapel to Astor Place and the Bowery to seek escape from the heat in the bosky grounds of the garden, whose gravel walks and ornate statuary were brilliantly illuminated by two thousand lamps. The theatre was located at the front entrance of the garden and staffed with some of the actors from the Park Theatre. Here for the first two nights of their engagement Eliza played Priscilla Tomboy and Rosina,[4] and David appeared as Frank in John Till Allingham's farce *Fortune's Frolic* and as Eliza's leading man Belville in *Rosina.*[5]

When they left New York not long after to continue their trip into New England, they had been married almost four months, and Eliza was pregnant.

It had been ten years since Eliza had been in Boston, but she would certainly have had vivid memories of its familiar landmarks, for they were her first impressions of America: the golden-domed State House, the Memorial Tower on cone-shaped Beacon Hill, and the grassy and wooded expanses of the Common where cows still grazed. There was also the smell of the sea and the sight of scores of ships in the huge harbor, which was visible from almost anywhere in town and which, with the Charles River, almost made Boston an island. Eliza would also have remembered State Street, where she and her mother had had lodgings,[6] and which was now the main thoroughfare of Boston and fast becoming the national symbol of new Federalist power and wealth. In sharp contrast to the older wooden buildings from Boston's Puritan past, the new brick buildings she now saw on State Street and the residences on Park Street and Beacon Hill reflected a growing taste for elegance among the populace,[7] a taste not only expressed in the exquisite Federal style, but also, Eliza and David would learn, in the kinds of plays that interested the Boston public.

None of Eliza's memories of Boston could have been more vivid than the old Federal Street Theatre where she had begun her life as an actress, but she and David would not be playing in this same theatre. It had burned in February 1798 and had been rebuilt and reopened the following October, redesigned by its original architect, Charles Bullfinch. Though the new theatre was improved acoustically, its facade was altered, and it did not have the colonnaded portico,

Corinthian pilasters, and Palladian windows of the original structure. The new Federal Street Theatre in Franklin Place was now the only theatre in Boston, the Haymarket having been sold at auction and dismantled in 1803.

It is ironic that J. T. Buckingham, whose reviews would so profoundly affect David's and Eliza's lives that season, was one of the first Boston writers to call the public's attention to her. In an article listing the new members of the company Buckingham remembered that "Mrs. Poe is the daughter of Mrs. Arnold, formerly of the Boston Theatre," and he added, "We understand she is to fill the parts made vacant by the departure of Mrs. Darley."[8] Following Mrs. Darley would mean important assignments for Eliza, even if pleasing Boston audiences in some of the same roles Mrs. Darley had played would be difficult. Ellen Darley, the former Ellen Westray, had been one of the leading actresses at the Federal Street Theatre for the last four seasons, and she was a popular favorite, especially of the much feared Buckingham, the publisher and reviewer of a new literary magazine called *The Polyanthos*.

Eliza and David both undoubtedly realized they were facing a highly critical audience. In the twelve years since Boston had opened its first theatre in 1794, its public had seen the finest actors in America. Fennell, Cooper, Mrs. Merry, and Jefferson had all played there regularly. Moreover, the Boston public was a highly literate one, and in its seven biweekly newspapers and two literary magazines Bostonians read detailed criticisms of all of the actors' work at the Federal Street Theatre. There were plenty of anonymous and prolific reviewers to fill the columns. It is true that few of these writers could be in any way considered professional critics, but they nonetheless affected the public's thinking, and every actor knew that winning their approval was important.

The opening weeks of rehearsals must have been tense ones. Both David and Eliza were, for the most part, working with strangers. David knew no one; he was a neophyte among old pros, a native American in a company composed mainly of transplanted Englishmen. Eliza did know Charlotte and Luke Usher from her days in the Chestnut Street Theatre, but she was acquainted with few, if any, of the other actors in the large company she and David had joined. They both knew John Bernard, but he was away in England in search of actors and new productions, and his ship had not arrived back in Boston in time for rehearsals.

During rehearsals Eliza and David discovered that they were members of a company nearly twice as large as that of the Virginia Company, with a repertory that was far more varied, particularly in Shakespeare's plays and the English comedy of manners. It was a repertory that reflected the keen interest Bostonians had in the spoken word, for in a town of eminent statesmen and preachers, oratory and elocution were naturally of great importance. That passionate supporter of the Boston Theatre, Robert Treat Paine (one of the first American writers to pay serious attention to the theatre and the art of acting), had often reminded the public that it was in the theatre that standards for the "force of elocution and purity of pronunciation"[9] were most effectively upheld, and that the plays of the classical English repertory contained the finest examples of language written to be spoken. At the Federal Street Theatre Eliza and David would be cast in classical plays to an extent neither of them had before. This must have especially interested David, because he had been most successful in poetic plays. It meant, however, that from the start they would both have to study and learn a great many new roles.

It must have added pressure to their work during the already tense rehearsals when they found they were both scheduled to make their debuts on the opening night of the season, and in leading roles. There was to be no gradual exposure: they were the front runners. The play was Thomas Morton's comedy *Speed the Plow,* a play they had both done with the Virginia Company. In one sense this was fortunate, because they knew the play well. David had often played Henry, the young hero around whose identity the plot centers, and Eliza had played Suzan, the ingenue. There is no record, however, of Eliza's having ever played Emma Blandford, the leading lady and heroine with whom Henry is in love, and it was in this role that the Boston managers cast her; so that Eliza probably had to make her first appearance before the Boston public in a role that was new to her repertoire.

The opening night was 13 October. Fortunately, the performance went well, and Eliza and David had a good, if somewhat guarded, reception in the press. In *The Polyanthos* J. T. Buckingham wrote:

> The parts of Henry and Miss Blandford were filled by Mr. and Mrs. Poe from the Virginia theatres, their first appearance in Boston. Estimating the talents of this couple by comparison, we might say the same characters have been more ably sustained on our boards. A first performance however does not always afford a criterion by which merit may be estimated. Mr. Poe possesses a full manly voice, of considerable extent; his utterance clear and distinct. The managers will undoubtedly find him a useful, and the town a pleasing, performer in the Henrys, Charles Stanleys, etc. Of the talents of Mrs. Poe we are disposed to judge favorably. [10]

It was evident that they were facing a demanding audience, and they would have to work hard. They did. In the first fourteen weeks of the season they both played more than twenty parts.

Eliza was assigned fourteen roles new to her repertoire—sometimes more than one new part a week. The management introduced her in the afterpieces and sentimental plays with considerable success. She made a hit as Priscilla Tomboy in *The Romp,* and as a result this play was given extra performances. The reviewer from the literary magazine *The Emerald* compared her "excellent" performance as the hoydenish Priscilla with that of the celebrated Louisa Fontenelle Williamson. [11] "I was extremely pleased with Mrs. Poe in Priscilla Tomboy," wrote another reviewer in *The Polyanthos*, "Many of her wanton tricks to tease her gawkish cousin Watty were truly laughable, and perhaps not the less so for being pretty correct representations of the manners of some of our country hoydens."[12] The critics also admired her singing, and in reviewing the new members of the company, a writer for the newspaper the *New England Palladium* singled her out for special praise: "The additions to the company have more than a respectable portion of talent; and Mrs. Poe in particular exhibits a flattering promise of very handsome ability in the lines of *naivete* comedy and the opera."[13]

With David, unfortunately, it was a different story. The reviewers found him talented and attractive, with a good voice and excellent natural equipment, but not yet a polished performer. One reviewer complained of his diction, another of his tameness, another of his mannerisms. He was unable to relax and avoid rushing and was consequently still having some trouble with memory. His shortcomings were in the main due to his lack of experience. He was working hard, and the management, who had confidence in his abilities, was casting him well, but his reception in the press was not encouraging. He was still struggling through a tough apprenticeship. Not all criticism was adverse. "He certainly possesses talent, which merits cultivation,"[14] wrote the critic for the newspaper the *Columbian Centinel*, and even *The Polyanthos* praised his performance as Maurice in James Cobb's musical drama *The Wife of Two Husbands*, but for every good notice there seemed to be two bad ones.

David had been a professional actor less than three years, and in the ruthless exposure he and Eliza had during the opening fall weeks of the season at the Federal Street Theatre his lack of experience showed. He was simply not as ready to face the Boston public as Eliza was. She had had ten years of steady work and carefully guided apprenticeship behind her, during which she had been gradually prepared to play longer and more demanding roles. David had not had this kind of training. From the very beginning of his career he had plunged immediately into the difficult parts. He was learning, but there had not been enough time for him to acquire the technique he lacked, and his instincts were not strong enough to carry him through.

It was a discouraging situation that could not have added to his peace of mind nor to the happiness of his home life with Eliza. Even with the most generous of spirits a marriage between actors can rarely be free of all professional jealousy, and Eliza seemed to be achieving all the success. There was also less time for her to give David the kind of attention he desperately needed to bolster his ego. Aside from her own heavy workload, she had been nearly five months pregnant at the beginning of the season and by December her time was close. It had been easy for her to conceal her pregnancy under the high-waisted Empire gowns, but the energy required to play the kind of spirited roles in which the managers cast her and in which she was achieving her success must have taken its toll on her strength and turned much of her attention away from David toward herself and the baby she was carrying.

She continued playing even during the last weeks of her pregnancy, through the Christmas holidays and into the beginning of the year until mid-January. Two weeks later, on 30 January, she gave birth to a son, whom she and David named William Henry.[15] On the night of his son's birthday David played Tressel to Thomas Cooper's Richard III. This was his second association with Cooper, who seems to have taken an interest in him, and during Cooper's six-night guest engagement at the Federal Street Theatre David had the opportunity to gain some ground with the public by appearing in the kind of poetic roles in which he had been most successful, among them Laertes in *Hamlet,* Malcolm in *Macbeth,* and Paris in *Romeo and Juliet.*

Unfortunately, however, his luck did not hold. Directly after Cooper's engagement ended and with very little notice David had to replace the actor who was to play Charles Surface in *The School for Scandal.* Such eleventh-hour casting assignments were inevitable with the constant change of plays in repertory, and to an experienced actor they posed a less serious problem than to David. There is no record of his having ever played Charles before, so it was probably a new part for him, and he was, moreover, performing with actors whose forte was the comedy of manners. John Bernard, who by now had returned to the company from England, and Mrs. Stanley, a well-known English actress whom Bernard had engaged in London, were both in leading roles in this production, and both of them had made their reputations playing high comedy. The critic for the *Columbian Centinel* called their performances "a picture of courtly life, manners, and conversation."[16] For David to succeed alongside them, especially in Federalist Boston, required him to understand and project a life-style to which he had never been exposed. He was evidently not very convincing, and he and Eliza had to read yet another discouraging notice. "We are ready to make allowances for Mr. Poe's deficiency in Sir Charles Surface, in manners, spirit, and orthoepy," wrote the reviewer for *The Emerald.* "The suddenness with which the character must have been assumed is a mantle, which like charity, covers a multitude of sins."[17]

In the meantime, Eliza had been out of the repertory and at home with her new baby. There had been time for a short rest, but she was soon back at work, exactly three and a half weeks after Henry's birth. The weeks following must have been a difficult time for her. She had to begin work on two long parts, and her new baby added a constant and exhausting responsibility that would have rarely let her sleep through the night. Life at home was bound to have become pressured, and David's frustrations could not have helped to ease the tensions.

Of the two new roles Eliza was learning, Cordelia was by far the more important assignment, for it meant that she would appear for the first time in her career with James Fennell, who along with Thomas Cooper stood at the head of the acting profession in America. Fennell was thirty-nine years old and at the height of his fame. Of Welsh and Scotch-Irish ancestry, he had made his American debut under Wignell and had quickly and steadily risen in popularity. He was a commanding figure, over six feet—at that time an unusually tall height—more than "two yards of man" his rival Thomas Cooper once described him. Fennell's gigantic figure, which towered over Eliza's, lacked grace, and he was not a versatile actor, never succeeding as a comedian, but he had an excellent voice and a superb command of spoken language. A mercurial and eccentric personality and a heavy drinker, he had been well educated at Eton and Cambridge, where he had been in training for the church, but he had left the university to become in turn, lawyer, inventor, editor, playwright, and teacher, though it was as an actor that he made his most enduring reputation.

The altered version of *King Lear* that was used in Eliza's day, and in which she would have appeared with Fennell, was very much unlike Shakespeare's play.[18] The plot was completely changed, and characters were added, rewritten, and eliminated. On the whole the play was shortened, and the moral tone so important to eighteenth- and nineteenth-century sensibilities was retained at the expense of the tragedy. Right, therefore, prevails, and Lear and Cordelia both survive, Cordelia to marry Edgar and become queen! Despite the vast differences in the text, nearly all of what Shakespeare wrote for Cordelia remained in the altered version and a number of speeches and scenes in which she appears were added, making the role considerably longer than it is in the original and requiring a stronger and more sustained performance. It was considered a major role, and Mrs. Siddons had played it in London. In playing Cordelia in Boston, Eliza was following the well-known favorite, Ellen Darley.

The opening of *King Lear* was announced for the week after Eliza's return to the Federal Street Theatre, but on the performance night preceding the scheduled opening, Fennel sprained his ankle and was ordered by his doctor to remain in bed for a week.[19] Since this was his first attempt at Lear, he was relieved to have the extra week for study—as were undoubtedly the other actors including Eliza.

On the night of the canceled *King Lear,* the management substituted George Lillo's popular play *The London Merchant,* and they cast David in the leading role of George Barnwell. It was a part that he had often played with the Virginia Company and also earlier that season in Boston. The play is described by its author as a domestic tragedy, and it tells the story of a young merchant driven to theft and finally murder as the result of his affair with an older woman. It is an excellent part, but again David was thrown into a major role at the last minute, and this time he had to face a public that had expectations of seeing Fennell as Lear. "Of Mr. Poe's Barnwell we expected little satisfaction, and of course were not disappointed,"[20] wrote J. T. Buckingham in *The Polyanthos,* quite evidently content to be displeased and expressing the disappointment he shared with a large segment of the public in having to wait to see Fennell's Lear.

The repertory continued, the public's impatient expectation of Fennell's Lear notwithstanding, and Eliza next appeared as Little Pickle in *The Spoiled Child.* It was her first appearance in this role before the Boston public; and since Little Pickle was the kind of juvenile role she had been trying hard to grow out of, she had not played it in more than two years. She would have naturally felt some nervousness in getting up in the part after so long a time, but surely she was totally unprepared for the kind of notice that appeared in *The Polyanthos*. "Mrs. Poe," wrote J. T. Buckingham, "was a very green Little Pickle. We never knew before that the *Spoiled Child* belonged to that class of being termed hermaphroditical, as the uncouthness of his costume seemed to indicate."[21]

In an age of careful propriety this kind of insult would have been difficult to swallow in the best of circumstances, but in Eliza's exhaustive situation it must have been devastating. Living with David through a very trying time had been a constant strain on her energies all season, and along with her added responsibilities at home she had just plunged headlong into a full and exhausting work schedule at the theatre. There had been little time for her to rest and adjust to the profound emotional changes that were taking place in her life since Henry's birth. It was an especially vulnerable time for her, and her resources for coping with the resentment and hurt and frustration she must have felt in being the butt of this kind of cheap journalism were at a low ebb.

David, stung by the tone of his own earlier notices in *The Polyanthos* and enraged at this last crack at Eliza, called on Buckingham personally to object to what he justly felt was impertinent and rude criticism.[22] Buckingham's attitude was aloof and patronizing, and David left, having done himself and Eliza more harm than good.

As the night of Fennell's Lear drew near, Eliza had good reason to feel uneasy. Not only would this be her first important appearance in Boston in poetic tragedy, but it was only the second time in her career that she had played a leading Shakespearean role, the last having been Ophelia at the Southwark in Philadelphia more than five years earlier. There had also been some worrisome publicity in one of the newspapers. Shortly after it was known to the public that Fennell was to play Lear, a writer for the *Columbian Centinal*, a Federalist newspaper, expressed the opinion that "as Mrs. Darley performed Cordelia, her absence leaves that character at the disposal of the managers to be allotted to Mrs. Stanley."[23] It was evidently known in Boston that Mrs. Stanley had played Cordelia in London, and many Bostonians expected to see her in the part instead of Eliza. It is true that she may have given the role more weight and authority than Eliza, but Eliza was nearer the right age—she was twenty—and could project the youth and artless, unaffected honesty so vital to the character of Lear's youngest daughter.

Eliza was understandably very nervous on the opening night of *King Lear*. It was difficult enough for her to follow Ellen Darley, but she also had to face an audience at least a part of which expected Mrs. Stanley as Cordelia. In writing of her performance, the reviewer for the *Columbian Centinel* sensed her uneasiness.

Of Mrs. Poe in Cordelia we would speak with the strictest delicacy and tenderness. Her amiable timidity evidently betrayed her own apprehension, that she had wandered from the sphere of her appropriate talent; while her lovely gentleness pleaded strongly for protection against the rigid justice of criticism. She was so obviously exiled from her own element by the mere humor of authority that we cannot in charity attempt any analysis of her performance.

This same writer wondered at some length why Mrs. Stanley had not been cast as Cordelia, but he ended his review by praising one aspect of Eliza's performance: "Mrs. Poe had one credit and that of no mean value—she did not mutilate the language of Shakespeare."[24] In *The Polyanthos* J. T. Buckingham took his revenge for David's visit in a characteristic jibe: "We know not which is more laughable, the absurd, preposterous conduct of the managers in giving the character of Cordelia to a lady who is so totally inadequate to its representation; or to the ridiculous vanity which prompted her to accept it."[25] The reviewer for *The Emerald*, however, had qualified praise: "Cordelia by Mrs. Poe, was interesting but the part is not suited to her voice." And of her second performance the following week he wrote: "Mrs. Poe as Cordelia, has once received our approbation, and has again deserved it. But we notwithstanding prefer her comedy."[26]

As a whole the production was a hit, and it was held over for three extra performances. However unsatisfying her experience or disappointing her reception, Eliza nonetheless had the distinction of having played Cordelia to Fennell's first Lear, and in appearing with him she had taken an important step in building a national reputation for herself.

During this time David had been appearing regularly in the repertory. Fennell played basically the same line of parts as Cooper, and David had been cast in some of the same supporting roles he had played earlier in the season with Cooper (notably Malcolm and Laertes, among others), thus alternating these parts in a single season with the two most eminent actors in America.

By now it was already late in the season, and benefits began. On John Bernard's night Eliza played Ariel in *The Tempest* for the first time in her career. Prospero's airy, "tricksy spirit" was a part for which she was uniquely suited and in which she must have been very good. Like *King Lear*, this production of *The Tempest* would also have been the altered version of Shakespeare's play, with cuts and added characters, but enough of the original survived to give her excellent scenes, and she had all but one of Ariel's songs as well as additional ones in which she was accompanied by a chorus of spirits and furies. Her friend Luke Usher, whom she had known since her days at the Chestnut Street Theatre, played Prospero; Bernard was Stephano; and David played the young hero Ferdinand.

The season ended on 25 May, no doubt for Eliza with a great sigh of relief.[27] Although she had achieved some success with the Boston public, especially as a comedienne, it had been for the most part a time of struggle, frustration, and disappointment. It must also have been psychologically and physically exhausting. She had never worked so hard. In all, she had added thirty-five new roles to her repertoire, almost as many as she had learned during her entire association with the Virginia Company, while at home for more than half the season she had had the constant responsibility of caring for Henry. All of this had deeply affected and changed her life with David. Together they must have faced the close of the season with mixed feelings. They certainly welcomed a break from the pressure of rehearsals and performances, but on the other hand their feelings of relief must have been tinged with some apprehension about the future. Where did they stand with the managers and the public? After all, they had had to face up to some very harsh criticism of their work. About the management, however, they need not have worried: they were both invited to return to the Federal Street Theatre for the following season.

They now had no commitments until the fall. This was the first time that Eliza had had this kind of break in her professional engagements since she was nine years old, and she must have looked forward to a much needed rest and vacation. It was most probably during this summer break that she and David first visited his parents in Baltimore. Henry was General Poe's first grandson, and he and his wife, now reconciled with David, welcomed Eliza for the first time in her life into a family circle outside the theatre. Writing many years later of Eliza's and David's first visit to the Poe home, David's older sister Maria, then seventeen and later the Maria Clemm who would become so important in Edgar Poe's life, remembered Eliza well: "She was a lovely little creature and highly talented. I loved her most devotedly."[28] For the next few years a visit to Baltimore would become a regular off-season trip for Eliza and David, and for Henry, who was to become a favorite of his grandparents, it was eventually home.

In the early fall Eliza and David were back in Boston ready to begin their second season at the Federal Street Theatre. Rehearsals began under far less pressure than they had the previous year. They were no longer working with strangers, and they were well acquainted with the company's repertory. During the summer there had been ample time for Eliza to rest, and she and David had also had time to begin adjusting to Henry's presence in their lives; but perhaps their greatest worry about the new season dissolved when they learned that *The Polyanthos* had folded, and they no longer needed to worry about J. T. Buckingham's acid pen.

There were still other Boston reviewers that they would have to please, but they might have learned something about the credibility of newspaper criticism at that time from an incident that occurred early in the season. An Englishman named Cromwell had presented the managers at the Federal Street Theatre a glowing set of press notices about his work in England, on the strength of which they had hired him. It eventually turned out, however, to the great embarrassment of the managers, that Cromwell himself had written these notices and submitted them anonymously to the editors of the English newspapers who had published them. Though he had fooled the managers, Cromwell could not fool the Boston public, which knew an imposter when it saw one, and soon his every appearance onstage was greeted with hissing, stamping, and outspoken abuse. The managers were forced to release him,[29] and in order to mollify their outraged public they brought back James Fennell for a rather extended guest engagement. Eliza and David both appeared frequently with Fennell during this engagement, often in the same roles they had played with him the preceding season, but Eliza's most important new assignement with him was Ophelia.

It had been more than five years since she had first played Ophelia at the old Southwark Theatre in Philadelphia. She had been fourteen then, but now, at twenty-two, she was technically far better equipped for the part and much nearer the right age. Most important of all, her experience as an actress and as a human being had deepened. It was her playing of the nunnery scene that most struck the critic for *The Emerald*: "Mrs. Poe was considerably moved at being sent by a lover to a nunnery. She did justice to the scene."[30] This same reviewer also found her mad scenes, enhanced by her skills as a singer, well played and interesting.

Audiences must have found something appealing in the contrast between the eloquent heaviness that distinguished Fennell's performances and the delicate and lyric lightness of Eliza's figure and personality, because the management cast her in two more important roles with him. She was Rosamunda of Corfu, "the loveliest maiden in Venice,"[31] in William Dunlap's translation of Heinrich Zschokke's romantic play *Abaellino,* in which Fennell made love to her as the hero Floradora and in disguise as the great bandit Abaellino. And in the altered version of *The Merchant of Venice* she played Jessica to his Shylock, speaking most of the lines that Shakespeare wrote. She also had a solo and a duet with Lorenzo, both of which were added to the original text, and she sang "Tell me where is fancy bred" in the Bassanio-casket scene, giving her somewhat more to do than Jessica has in Shakespeare's play of the same title.

David and Eliza were appearing often, both with Fennell and in other plays in the repertory; and since there were fewer new assignments for either of them, they were relatively free from the pressure of learning and rehearsing new roles. There was more time for them to spend together, and their life was far less hectic than it had been the preceding season. Moreover, the discouraging and disheartening notices that David had had to read about his work had begun to be replaced with more encouraging ones. Though the critic for *The Emerald* disliked David's performance of Malcolm and complained that as Vernon in Shakespeare's *Henry IV,* he had "mutilated some of his speeches in a most shameful manner,"[32] it was not long before this same critic was writing more favorably. "Mr. Poe in Norfolk," he observed in reviewing the company's production of Shakespeare's *Henry VIII,* "was courtly in manners, if he was not perfect in his delivery,"[33] and finally, of David's performance in Nicholas Rowe's tragedy *The*

*Fair Penitent,* he wrote, "Poe was perfect in his part and made quite a tolerable Altamont. He played best the first scene with Horatio."[34]

The week following Fennell's engagement, the managers brought in Mrs. Warren as the second special guest star of the season. Mrs. Warren was the former Ann Brunton Merry, widow of Thomas Wignell and now married to William Warren. Eliza and David both appeared with her during the seven nights of her engagement. Not since Eliza's days as an ingenue in Wignell's company had she been associated with this great actress, whom many of her contemporaries considered the equal of Sarah Siddons. Mrs. Warren began her engagement at the Federal Street Theatre by playing a line of heroines from the poetic tragedies in which she had made her brilliant reputation and that were so popular with early nineteenth-century audiences.[35] They are now all but forgotten names and titles: Belvidera in Thomas Otway's *Venice Preserved,* Elvira in Richard Brinsley Sheridan's verse adaptation of August von Kotzebue's *Pizarro,* Euphrasia in Arthur Murphy's *The Grecian Daughter,* and the title role in Thomas Southerne's *Isabella.* In her only appearance in a comedy she played Lady Teazle, and she closed her engagement as Calista in *The Fair Penitent* and Juliet in *Romeo and Juliet* with James Fennell as her co-star in both productions. Eliza was featured in several of the afterpieces during Mrs. Warren's engagement but was actually in only one play with her, as the young mother Cora in the Sheridan-Kotzebue *Pizarro.* This was an important role, however, requiring her to sustain an intense and highly emotional pitch throughout the play.

Toward the beginning of December Eliza began rehearsals for the most successful production with which she was ever connected. This was *Cinderella,* one of those extraordinary pantomimes that were then so popular. Rehearsals were under the direction of Sr. Cipriani, the choreographer whom Bernard had brought back with him from England.

*Cinderella* was a lavishly spectacular production with "new and splendid scenery, machinery, dresses, and decorations."[36] The machinery and costumes were made in England, but the new scenery was painted by the company's own scene painter, James Warrell. Both Eliza and David were assigned parts. David was cast as the Prince, and in the allegorical scenes with the gods, interpolated into the familiar story of the old fairy tale, Eliza was cast as Venus. Both roles were central ones. David appeared throughout with Charlotte Usher, who played Cinderella, and as Venus, Eliza was involved in the plot throughout the story. Besides the songs she had, she also spoke lines written in poetry and recitative. Cipriani himself appeared in the role of Pedro, the servant to Cinderella's sisters. The production effects, done within the representational style in which all spectacle was presented at that time, were enormously complicated and required careful rehearsal. In all there were eleven scenes, among them the summit of Mount Ida and the bower of Venus, a night scene in the Garden of Venus, the illuminated palace and ballroom, and a palace in the clouds for the wedding of Cinderella and the Prince at the altar of Hymen with

flying Cupids and Graces. To the delight of audiences there were several transfor-
mation scenes accomplished by the simultaneous and sudden change of all the
flats onstage, and the machinery included not only flown props and actors but
also a pedestal that changed into a sofa, a dresser that became a toilette, and a
rosebush that was miraculously transformed into a car into which Cupid
mounted and ascended to the clouds. Besides these effects there were, of course,
the pumpkin that became a coach and the white mice that were changed into
horses. It is important to remember that all of these devices were accomplished
within current theatrical conventions and for an audience that had no taste for
realism. Realism was yet unborn, a hundred years in the future. Nonetheless the
smooth performance of *Cinderella* required skillful teamwork on the part of the
actors and the crew as well, and the limited rehearsal and performance schedule
under which everyone was working imposed an even stricter than usual discipline on the rehearsals. *Cinderella* opened on 7 December and was immediately
an enormous hit. It took an important place in the repertory and played through
Christmas. Audiences crowded to see it, making it necessary to schedule eleven
performances.[37]

The same month that *Cinderella* opened at the Federal Street Theatre,
Congress passed the Embargo Act, forbidding American exports to Europe.
Since Boston was one of the largest shipping centers in the country, idle ships
began to crowd its harbor, and it must have been during this embargo that one
morning Eliza had the time to walk down to the harbor, then more than usually
crowded with ships, and make a sketch of the many vessels lying at bay in the
huge body of water surrounding the city. Underneath this sketch she wrote
"Morning 1808." She kept her drawing and in time eventually inscribed it with
one of the few personal records of her short life: "for my little son Edgar, who
should ever love Boston the place of his birth and where his mother found her
best and most sympathetic friends."[38] That season of 1808–9 in Boston, when
she was most free from the pressures at home and at the theatre, when she was
making close friends in the company and she and David were finally beginning
to gain a good following with the public, must have been one of the happiest and
most tranquil times of her life.

Meantime the repertory at the Federal Street Theatre continued but to
dwindling audiences, because the embargo hit Boston particularly hard, and
everyone there felt the economic pinch. The managers turned to guest stars, and
when they brought in the popular comedian William Twaits from New York to
play Dr. Pangloss in George Colman II's *The Heir at Law,* they cast Eliza as Cicely
Homespun. This was a new role for her and the opportunity to appear before the
Boston public as an artless and ingenuous country girl with a background far
removed from the tragic heroines and well-bred young ladies of fortune with
whom she had most often been identified that season. The reviewer for *The
Emerald* felt that she played Cicely with "spirit and force," and he also found
David "respectable" as Henry Morland, the young leading man.[39]

The managers now brought in Thomas Cooper, and they cast Eliza as his Ophelia, Cordelia, and Jessica, giving her the enviable opportunity, as David had had the previous season, of playing the same parts in the same season with the country's two most eminent actors. Though she had worked with Cooper in Virginia, she had never played these roles with him. Eliza found him vastly different in temperament and approach from Fennell, who was far more consistent and disciplined. Cooper was an erratic, spontaneous, and truly brilliant performer, but he was unfortunately also a careless study. This was surely unnerving for Eliza, but she nonetheless must have found playing with him exciting. Cooper had an enviable reputation in both England and America, and Washington Irving, who spent many years as a theatregoer on both sides of the Atlantic, felt that Cooper's Macbeth was unequaled anywhere in the English-speaking world.[40]

After Cooper's engagement had ended and the closing weeks of the season drew near, business again fell off, and the managers seem to have been in a quandry as to how to capture the public's fancy. One night Eliza and David even found themselves on the same bill with ten Oneida Indians! In a less exotic attempt at novelty, however, the management finally decided to mount a number of new productions, and in the last six playing weeks of the season Eliza learned almost as many new parts as she had all season.

One of these parts was Cora, the heroine of Frederick Reynolds's version of Kotzebue's drama *The Virgin of the Sun*. Cora is an Inca princess in love with the Spanish conquistador Alonzo. The hero of the play is Rolla, formerly a general of the Peruvian army. The story of Rolla, Alonzo, and Cora was a very popular one, and three plays had been written about it. Eliza, thoroughgoing professional that she was, now had all three versions in her repertoire. She played this new role for hers and David's benefit, and on the day their benefit was announced the *Gazette* published an editorial about her work.

If industry can claim from the public either favor or support, the talents of Mrs. Poe will not pass unrewarded. She has supported and maintained a course of characters, more numerous and arduous than can be paralleled on our boards, during any one season. Often she has been obliged to perform three characters on the same evening, and she has always been perfect in the text, and has well comprehended the intention of her author.

In addition to her industry, however, Mrs. Poe has claims for other favors, from the respectability of her talents. Her romps and sentimental characters have an individuality which has marked them peculiarly her own. But she has succeeded often in the tender personations of tragedy; her conceptions are always marked with good sense and natural ability.

We hope, therefore, that when the united recommendations of the talents of both Mr. and Mrs. Poe are put up for public approbation, that that public will not only not discountenance virtuous industry and exertion to please, but will stretch forth the arm of encouragement to cheer, to support, and to save.[41]

However satisfying it was for Eliza to read such a sympathetic appreciation of her work, the good publicity unfortunately failed to help attract a large house, and she and David gave their benefit at a loss. They were still entitled to another benefit, however, and they decided to try their luck in a joint venture with their friends Charlotte and Luke Usher, who had also just had an unsuccessful benefit. As the plays they chose Friedrich Schiller's famous tragedy about petty tyrrany, *The Robbers*, and a play that had never been performed in the United States, James Kenney's *Ella Rosenberg*. Eliza, now described in *The Emerald* as the "favorite of the public and the delight of the eye"[42] was cast as the heroine in both these plays.

Though *The Robbers* is infinitely stronger and psychologically far more complex, both it and *Ella Rosenberg* are essentially melodrama, the style of play that during Eliza's lifetime was becoming increasingly popular. These early melodramas were tightly and neatly constructed and played briskly before swiftly changing scenery. All of the situations were totally unrealistic and devised primarily to create big moments for the actors to fill. Their effectiveness depended far less upon the realistic or logical development and portrayal of character than it did upon the vivid pictures and impressions it left on the audience's imagination, and in order for Eliza to succeed in them, she had to play them with bold and full-blooded commitment. There is no record to tell whether or not the Poes and Ushers succeeded in regaining their losses by their joint effort. If they did, they were luckier than the managers, who closed the season on 25 April after thirty playing weeks and at a loss for the second year running.[43]

## 13

## Roscius

THE LONG SUMMER MONTHS of 1808 must have been lean ones for Eliza and David. The losses they had suffered at their benefit had probably left them short of money, and although they had both signed for the coming fall and winter season at the Federal Street Theatre, there was little work to be had until then. The embargo had tightened the strings on the public's pocketbook, and those managers who had not been forced to close their theatres were only barely making expenses and consequently keeping their payrolls to a minimum. It was hardly a comforting state of affairs for two unemployed young actors with a small baby to provide for—and their worries about the future could only have increased as Eliza learned that she was beginning her second pregnancy.

For at least part of that summer they were in the Richmond and Petersburg area, where they did manage to find some work. Both their names appear in an advertisement for a performance of John Brown's *Barbarossa* in Petersburg on 29 June. This was an important night for Eliza, who, continuing to add to her stock of tragic roles, played Irene, one of the leading parts.[1] It was the first time she had played in an early eighteenth-century tragedy, a style of play with which she was familiar mostly from having often played in Henry Fielding's hilarious burlesque of this genre, *The Tragedy of Tragedies*. Two weeks after this Petersburg performance she and David were in Richmond, where with two other actors from Boston they appeared at the Haymarket Garden.[2]

These meagre facts are all that is definitely known about those five months of Eliza's life. From later advertisements in the Petersburg papers[3] it appears that she and David may have remained in the Petersburg area for most of the summer, appearing from time to time with a number of their friends in cut versions of short plays or in miscellaneous entertainments, setting up performances wherever there might have been a stage and an audience. If so, it was risky work and even at best a precarious way to eke out a living until rehearsals began in Boston in September.

When they finally did return to Boston in the fall, greatly relieved to be sure that they were employed again, they began rehearsals in a refurbished theatre.[4]

The managers had repainted and embellished the lobby and interior of the Federal Street Theatre and, despite their losses of the previous season, had even added a new set of wing lamps to the stage. Theatre Alley fronting on the stage door had also been boarded up. Eliza would have been happy to see this, because the mire that had sometimes collected there had often made it embarrassingly necessary for her and the other actresses to enter the theatre from the front of the house to keep their long skirts from being drenched with the mud.

There were a number of changes in the acting company that season. Eliza's friends the Shaws and Ushers had left, as had Mrs. Stanley. Most conspicuous among the newcomers was the English actress Mrs. George Woodham,[5] who was a member of an American Tory family that had left the United States during the Revolution and who had recently returned, appearing with great success in Philadelphia and Charleston. She was a very skillful comedienne and dancer, and with her fair coloring and expressive features she made a striking figure on the stage. She played the same line of parts as Eliza, and during the season their assignments overlapped.

Eliza was five months pregnant when the season began, and she was evidently unable to assume a full workload. She did not make her first appearance of the season until the fourth week after the opening when she played Cordelia to Fennell's Lear, and for the following eleven weeks she was not assigned any new roles. In the meantime, Mrs. Woodham played Little Pickle, Moggy McGilpin, Cicely Homespun in *The Heir at Law*, and Variella in *The Woodcock*. These were all parts that had been previously assigned to Eliza but that her pregnancy must now have made it impossible for her to play because they were too strenuous.

Nonetheless, she still managed to appear regularly until early January when she left to have her baby. Within two weeks after she had stopped playing, on 19 January (the same time of year Henry had been born two years earlier), Eliza gave birth to her second son, whom she and David named Edgar. At the time they were living in Henry Haviland's house, located on an unnamed street south of the Common near the Charles River.[6] It must have been with mixed feelings that Eliza and David greeted the arrival of the child who was destined to become so great a writer. Edgar was an added responsibility to an already hectic professional life as well as yet another pressure to a marriage that by now had probably begun to show signs of serious trouble.

Three weeks after Edgar's birth Eliza was back on the stage again, and almost immediately after her return to the Federal Street Theatre, David's name disappears from the cast lists for nine straight weeks. Where he was at this critical time of Eliza's life is only partly known, as are so many of the facts that would throw light on the true and full story of this compulsive and talented young man. He was not in Boston for the whole time, however, for on 22 March he is known to have been in Stockerton, Pennsylvania (a small town between Philadelphia and Baltimore), where he visited his first cousin George, a well-to-do banker there. In a letter to William Clemm, Jr. (later David's brother-in-law), George Poe described David's rather mystifying visit.[7]

> You may have heard my father speak of a visit I had a few days ago from young Roscius. . . . One evening he came out to our house . . . he had me called out to the door where he told me the most awful moment of his life was arrived, begged me to come and see him the next day 11 o'clock at the Mansion House, said he came not to beg, and with a tragedy stride walked off after I without reflection promised I would call—in obedience to my promise I went there the next day but found him not nor did I hear of him until yesterday . . .

It is evident from George's attitude that the reconciliation that David had had with his mother and father after Henry's birth certainly did not extend to his cousins: "the young Roscius," George Poe calls him, not needing to identify him further. Whatever David's reason for not keeping his appointement at the Mansion House, he was still in Stockerton a week and a half later when he sent George the following note:

> Sir, you promised *me* on your honor to meet me at the Mansion House on the 23d—*I* promise *you* on *my* word of honor that if you will lend me, 30, 20, 15, or even 10$ I will *remit* it to you *immediately* on my arrival in Baltimore. Be assured I will keep *my* promise at least as well as you did yours and that nothing but extreme distress would have *forc'd* me to make this application— Your answer by the bearer will prove whether I yet have "favour in your eyes" or whether I am to be despised by (as I understand) a rich relation because when a wild *boy* I join'd a profession which I then thought and now think an honorable one. But which I would most willingly quit tomorrow if it gave satisfaction to your family provided I could do *any thing* else that would give bread to mine—Yr. politeness will not doubt induce you to answer this note from Yrs & c.
>
> D. Poe, Jr.[8]

Beneath these anxious and probably hastily written words it is possible to catch a fleeting glimpse of David's situation. It must have been a desperate time for him. He needed money, and it is plain he was worried about supporting his growing family and discouraged about his career. Perhaps his ambitions were beginning to give way to self doubt and uncertainty. He still resented some of his relatives' attitude toward him, and surely it was galling to have to ask his cousin for a loan. But why was he in Stockerton? Was he stranded there? And why, if he needed money so badly, did he leave his job in Boston for nine weeks? Had David been compelled by a reckless and unbalanced nature to run away from the problems he feared to face in Boston? And if so, what were these problems? How did they affect Eliza? And what was "the most awful moment of his life" of which he spoke? Intriguing questions to which George Poe's letter gives no answers.

To this impertinent note it is hardly necessary to tell you my answer—

the banker-cousin continues,

> it merely went to assure him that he need not look to me for any countenance or support more especially after having written me such a letter as that and thus for the future I desired to hear not of him—so adieu to Davy—

George Poe's reference to David as the "young Roscius" was not without calculated irony. All of the leading actors working in America at the time David became an actor had begun their careers in England. It is true that many of them became American citizens and spent most of their careers in the United States; but like all Americans they had an immigrant heritage, and by birth they were English. No native-born American actor had yet established himself as a star. The arrival of the American Roscius, as the popular phrase described this young national hero-to-be, was an eagerly awaited event, and it is not at all unlikely that David Poe had dreamed of achieving the distinction. This place in history was to fall, however, to a seventeen-year-old actor named John Howard Payne, a brilliant and handsome youth with glowing eyes and a melodious voice who first captivated American audiences at the Park Theatre in New York while David Poe was still on his unexplained journey to the south and whose meteoric rise to prominence would touch Eliza's career with important and to her altogether unexpected results.

Today it is rare and virtually impossible for a young actor to make his professional debut in a leading part, let alone a great one, but in the early nineteenth century it was standard practice. Managers thought little of bringing out a fledgling in a leading part and letting him sink or swim in the effort. The young actor may have lacked skill or maturity, as many critics were to note of John Howard Payne's first performances, but unlike his twentieth-century counterpart he did not want for abundant and challenging opportunities.

Accordingly, during three weeks in March at the Park Theatre, in his first appearances as a professional actor, John Howard Payne gave audiences a taste of his quality in six leading roles: as Young Norval in John Home's *Douglas*, as Octavian in George Colman II's *The Mountaineers*, as Achmet in John Brown's *Barbarossa*, as Tancred in James Thomson's *Tancred and Sigismunda*, as Zaphne in James Miller's translation of Voltaire's *Mahomet the Imposter*, and finally as Romeo in *Romeo and Juliet*. With the exception of *The Mountainers* and *Romeo and Juliet,* all of the plays were revivals from a generation earlier, mid-eighteenth-century poetic tragedies written in the neoclassical mold.

Payne's success was instantaneous, and word spread quickly that the American Roscius had arrived.

Benefits had already begun at the Federal Street Theatre in Boston when the 3 March edition of the *New England Palladium* carried news of his performances: "Master Payne, of this town, made his debut at the New York Theatre on Friday evening last in the character of Young Norval. He was much commended in the papers. At one time the applause of hands was seven times repeated." Bostonians knew John Howard Payne well, for he was the son of William Payne, a teacher of elocution and headmaster of the Berry Street Academy, a Boston boarding school located very near the Federal Street Theatre.

A management operating at a loss could not miss the opportunity of booking such a sure draw as Payne would be to the Boston public; and Powell, Dickenson, and Bernard—"sage, grave men,"[9] as Payne in his rather high-handed manner later called them—quickly entered into negotiations to bring the young Roscius to the Federal Street Theatre. They were able to secure him for a six-night engagement to begin immediately after Easter week, and they announced that he would make his Boston debut on 3 April as Norval in *Douglas,* with Mrs. Powell in the part of Lady Randolph.

Payne insisted that the managers cast him in the other plays with a leading lady that was petite in size, for though he had a vibrant and vital personality, his physique was small, and the managers, in an auspicious moment of fortune, chose Eliza Poe to play as his principal support.

By this time Eliza was an actress of considerable experience. She had worked hard at building a name for herself and had already appeared prominently with both Fennell and Cooper. Now, the opportunity of being Payne's leading lady could only further enhance her growing national reputation, for the new American Roscius had assumed an enormous importance to the public. Suddenly, for Eliza a season that had been comparatively inactive and routine took a completely unexpected turn, and she found herself not only standing squarely in the public eye but also facing an enormous workload.

The young Roscius had been engaged for six nights, and he was to play the same six roles he had appeared in at the Park Theatre. Eliza was cast in four of these plays—in long and difficult parts, only one of which she had played before. During the first week of Payne's engagement she was scheduled to appear with him as Palmyra in *Mahomet the Imposter* and in her first Juliet; in the second week she was to play Irene in *Barbarossa* (a role she had played the preceding summer in Petersburg) and Sigismunda in *Tancred and Sigismunda.* She was also cast in the afterpiece on his opening night, also in a new role.

Payne's engagement was scheduled to begin after Easter, and fortunately for Eliza the theatre was scheduled to close during Easter Week. This would have been a welcome break for her, because she needed all the time she could get. She had five roles to study, four of them new to her repertoire. An actress today would expect at least three weeks rehearsal for any one of them; Eliza had slightly more than three weeks for all five. David was evidently still away, and she had a three-month-old baby at home. This meant that she was still probably unable to sleep through the night. If Henry was with her, she also had a two-year-old to be taken care of. Her hands were full to say the very least. The physical and nervous strain of the next six weeks of her life must have been enormous: along with the constant responsibility of her two small sons she faced a task at the theatre that demanded a superbly trained actress with leonine courage and nerve.

John Howard Payne's Boston debut was treated by the management with ceremony appropriate to the taste of the public that filled the Federal Street Theatre on Monday, 3 April; Boston's poet, Robert Treat Paine, a distant cousin of John Howard Payne, was on hand to deliver an occasional address in verse. In the tragedy *Douglas,* the first play on the bill for the evening, there was no part for Eliza, but she did appear in the afterpiece, as the leading ingenue Emma in George Colman II's musical entertainment *We Fly by Night.*

Then two days later on Wednesday, 5 April, Eliza made her debut as Payne's leading lady when she played Palmyra in James Miller's translation of Voltaire's *Mahomet the Imposter.* Like all of the tragedies from the Age of Reason, this play has a highly moral theme; it tells a story of suppression and religious tyranny. The scene is Mecca, where Mahomet, supreme conqueror, prince, and pontiff, plots to have his zealous disciple Zaphna (the part played by Payne) kill a man whom Zaphna does not know is his own father. Palmyra, unknown to herself or Zaphna, is Zaphna's sister; she feels drawn to him by conflicting feelings she recognizes as those of both lover and sister. Also a follower of Mahomet, she reluctantly encourages Zaphna to obey their master's cruel command. After the murder, Zaphna and Palmyra both learn their true identities. Mahomet poisons Zaphna and then as a final indignity demands that Palmyra join his harem. Rather than submit to his treachery, she commits suicide. To succeed as Palmyra (one of Mrs Siddons's roles) Eliza had to project the turbulent and ambivalent feelings Palmyra has toward Zaphna, her father, and Mahomet, and she had to do so with an unfailing correctness and precision of articulation, for the play is written in highly formal verse.

However exciting this first appearance with Payne may have been for her, Eliza had little time, if any, to reflect on it, because on Friday of that same week, only two days later, she played Juliet to his Romeo. It was her first time in this great role, although she knew the play well and had by now seen a number of fine actresses play Juliet including Ann Merry, Anne West, and Elizabeth Powell. Many times and in many different theatres Eliza had danced in the masquerade scene and sung in the procession that, in the altered version used in her lifetime, occurs at Juliet's funeral in the beginning of the fifth act. This would have given her an opportunity to absorb some knowledge about the play and the part, but even so it meant that she had little more than a headstart in learning and playing one of the greatest and most difficult parts in the entire repertory. And she had to do it with highly pressured rehearsals.

As in all of her Shakespearean parts, Eliza would have played in the altered version of the play then in vogue. It included all of Juliet's great scenes and speeches, except that the fifth act was rewritten. Garrick, whose version was still popular in Eliza's day, had rewritten the last act to clear it of what he called its "jingle and quibble,"[10] so that, as Juliet, Eliza awoke in the tomb well before Romeo's death, and she and Payne had a long scene to play before finally dying in each other's arms.

When the first week of Payne's two-week engagement ended with the performance of *Romeo and Juliet*, Eliza faced a weekend in which she had to get up in the part of Irene for a Monday-night performance of John Brown's *Barbarossa*, adapted from Voltaire's *Mérope*. Fortunately, she had played this part the preceding summer in Petersburg. Again the play was an early eighteenth-century tragedy with an exotic setting, this time in Algiers, and again the theme was one of tyrany and family loyalty. As Irene, Eliza played Barbarossa's daughter in love with the hero Selim and torn between conflicts involving her father and her lover. Payne was in the role of Selim.

After playing Irene, Eliza was not scheduled to appear again with Payne for four days, but the pressure was still on. During those four days she had to learn and rehearse the role of Sigismunda in James Thomson's *Tancred and Sigismunda*—one of the truly great parts from the English neoclassical tragedies and another of Mrs. Siddons's roles. This play, set in Palermo among political turmoil and furious intrigue, is written in stately and graceful verse that combines correctness of form with moments of true lyricism. Eliza and Payne, again as star-crossed lovers, both had superb opportunities for bold, bravura acting of the first order, and Eliza had an excellent death scene.

In playing these eighteenth-century tragedies, Eliza had to work within a very strict style. The verse as well as the situations in these plays is highly formal. Moreover, her performance would have been further restricted by the costuming, because, traditionally, she would have been wearing heavy gowns and probably an elaborate headdress that would not have allowed her to use a great deal of movement.

After the performance of *Tancred and Sigismunda*, she could finally take a long, deep breath. The greatest pressures were off, but she had not, however, played her final performance with Payne. For his benefit on Monday, 17 April, he chose to play Hamlet, and she was his Ophelia, a part that by now she had done many times. In appearing as Payne's Ophelia, however, Eliza was taking part in an occasion of which she, the audience, and the other actors were all very keenly aware, because Payne was the first native American to play Hamlet.

David Poe played Laertes in this production. Sometime during the last hectic weeks of Eliza's life he had returned to Boston to discover that his young wife was achieving the first important success of her career and in partnership with the new American Roscius. It is doubtful that this discovery would have eased David's already confused state of mind. There was no part for him in Eliza's success. Perhaps, as the husband of a rising young actress, he even felt that his own career was to be very nearly eclipsed by hers. Eliza's appearances with Payne had certainly been of great personal importance to her, but how could David have avoided feeling envious of her association with an actor whose success and sudden fame had been in such marked contrast to the disappointment and struggle he had had to face?

However Eliza's newly won position in the public eye affected her life with David, she had nonetheless made a significant professional advance. It is true that Payne had been the main focus of attention, but her share of the limelight was not all reflected glory. Payne himself realized the excellent support she had given him, and as a gesture of his appreciation he agreed to stay on another night to appear with her for her benefit. He was not the only one to recognize Eliza's work. In announcing the play for her benefit, the *New England Palladium* printed the following editorial.

> Among the meritorious claimants for the patronage and liberality of a judicious public, we take peculiar pride and satisfaction in noticing Mrs. Poe. In their performances generally, few take precedence of this pleasing actress; and for their assiduity, accuracy, and unassuming deportment, with an uniform and studious desire to please, none. To the Boston stage she ever has been, and still is, a rich support; and for her unwearied exertions since the appearance of Master Payne, she certainly merits the highest commendation. The excellence of her Juliet, Sigismunda, Ophelia, etc., excited a lively interest and gratification in the beholders; and 'tis sincerely to be hoped that tomorrow evening they will not fail to reciprocate such an interest and gratification, in turn, as shall produce in her the warmest emotions of gratitude to a brilliant and overflowing house. The reward of merit alone must prove a sufficient inducement. When to these are united the charms of her Cora in Kotzebue's *Pizarro,* and the Rolla of Master Payne, which is his last appearance in Boston, we feel the utmost confidence in her success.[11]

This benefit probably did yield Eliza a much-needed profit.

By now the season was drawing to an end. Eliza appeared twice more with Payne (whom the managers persuaded to stay on beyond his announced engagement), but neither time in new roles. She played Amelia to his Federick in Kotzebue's *Lover's Vows,* and when James Fennell returned to play Lear with Payne as Edgar, Eliza was Cordelia. She played her last new role of the season on the next-to-last performance night, when she appeared as Marianna in James

Fennell's comedy *Lindor and Clara*. The season closed two nights later on 12 May.[12]

It had ended brilliantly for Eliza. She had achieved the first important recognition of her career. At the close of her third season at the Federal Street Theatre, she had established herself with the Boston public as both comedienne and tragedienne. She had played some of the great roles of poetic tragedy, and her repertoire now included the entire range available to an actress of her time. At twenty-three she seemed on the brink of coming into her own.

But what of David, and her life with him?

# "A Mere Mark to Shoot At"

DESPITE HER SUCCESSES in Boston, Eliza did not plan to stay at the Federal Street Theatre for another season. Both she and David had taken engagements with the management of Stephen Price and Thomas Cooper at the Park Theatre in New York. Rehearsals were to begin in the late summer for an early fall opening. It would mean a good long stretch of employment for them, because the season at the Park was longer than that at the Federal Street.

Meantime, after closing at the Federal Street Theatre on 12 May, Eliza, again taking advantage of the exposure she had had the last weeks of the season, remained in Boston to sing in a concert at the Exchange Coffee House,[1] and then she and David traveled to New York, where, with two other actors from the Boston Company, they planned to present another concert.[2]

However much they may have needed the added income this concert would have brought them, they were running a considerable risk in making any public appearance in New York before the fall. Their contract with Price and Cooper specifically forbade them to do so, and they were certainly mistaken if they thought their new managers would not hold them to their contract. As soon as he learned of their plans, Stephen Price notified them that should they appear in this concert he would enforce the stiff penalty provided for in their contract. Eliza and David were neither able nor willing to face this risk, and they left for Baltimore on the morning of the proposed performance.[3] Angry at being forsaken at the eleventh hour, the other actors announced in the *Commercial Advertiser* that the concert was canceled on account of the "sudden disappearance of Mrs. Poe."[4]

It must therefore have been with some uneasiness that Eliza and David returned to New York in August to begin rehearsals for their new managers. Stephen Price was a strict disciplinarian; and he would not have looked kindly upon their attempt to appear in New York in violation of their contract with him.

Unlike most theatrical managers of his time, Price was not an actor but a lawyer and businessman who had bought into the management at the Park Theatre in 1808 at the age of twenty-six. His interest in the theatre was strictly moneymaking. When Eliza and David first met him, he was just beginning his long and highly successful career as America's first theatrical magnate, making the Park Theatre pay as no one had before him. The son of a well-to-do New York merchant, and a graduate of Columbia College, he also had a taste for luxury and he and Thomas Cooper occupied adjoining houses on the corner of Broadway and Leonard Streets, where they both led active and brilliant social lives.

Of the two managers it was probably Cooper who had hired the Poes. By now they had both played with him often, and he knew their work well. This was the second time that Cooper had shown an interest in David's career, the first being his appearance as Glenalvon in David's Baltimore debut.

The Park Theatre, where the Poes began rehearsals with a company with whom for the most part they were not acquainted, stood on Park Row and towered over the adjacent buildings. Its wide steps extended the entire width of the three lots that the building occupied and led to seven arched doorways through which audiences entered the different parts of the house. The theatre was a large and imposing building facing City Hall Park and extending backward to Theatre Alley (which still exists today). It had opened in 1798 to replace the venerable John Street Theatre, where Eliza would have remembered appearing with her mother twelve years earlier. The Park contained a colonaded lobby warmed by fireplaces at either end, a large pit, three semicircular rows of boxes, and a gallery over the upper front boxes. Unlike many theatres at that time there were no pillars to obstruct the audience's view of the stage. The house had excellent acoustics and seated two thousand. It was the largest in the country. The stage combined a wide and rounded apron or forestage with a deep inner stage for the machinery and drops. Permanent doors opened onto the forestage.[5]

As David and Eliza began rehearsals, the management had just finished redecorating the theatre in airy and light colors. Fawn-colored panels surrounded by borders of gray, light purple, and white had been added to the fronts of the boxes. Gold columns and decoration adorned the molding and coves of the boxes, which the audience entered through rich mahogany doors. The walls of the theatre were painted and paneled in straw, pink, and light purple. There were also new chandeliers. A large and brilliant one hung from the dome; smaller ones flanked it on either side and were spread throughout the second- and third-tier boxes.[6]

The audiences that Eliza and David would face at the Park Theatre were often in marked contrast to the magnificence of the theatre's decor. Newspaper writers complained of the noisy gallery, of spectators standing on the benches in the pit; in describing a performance, one writer reported that the audience "was not guilty of any striking indecorum . . . excepting the throwing a fork at Mrs. Oldmixon"![7] Writing a few years earlier as Jonathan Oldstyle in the *Morning Chronicle*, Washington Irving had asserted that the Park audience itself was "no inconsiderable part of the entertainment," accustomed as it was to voicing its disapproval by "stamping, hissing, roaring, whistling, and . . . groaning in cadence," and at any moment begining a "discharge of apples, nuts, and gingerbread on the heads of the honest folks in the pit."[8] These audiences at the Park may have been a rowdy bunch, but they formed a homogeneous and enthusiastic public to whom Eliza and David, having both last appeared only very briefly at the Vauxhall Garden Theatre in New York, were virtually unknown. Then there were the critics to whom they were also strangers.

Whatever discouraging doubts David may still have had about his career and however they had affected his troubled life with Eliza, the new season at the Park Theatre was the opportunity for them both to make a fresh start. There was at least a chance that new and unfamiliar surroundings would bring them closer together and give them more in common. The challenge of working with different actors and playing for new audiences might have been an opportunity for them both to share important professional gains.

The season started well enough. Although opening night had originally been announced for 30 August, it was postponed until 6 September on account of the redecoration of the theatre. Eliza and David were cast in both opening plays. Eliza, again making a first appearance to an unfamiliar public in a role that was new to her repertoire, played the gentle and timid heroine Angela in Matthew G. Lewis's romantic thriller, *The Castle Spectre*. David played the embittered African slave Hassan. In the afterpiece Eliza played Priscilla in *The Romp* and David was Capt. Sprightly. The anonymous critic for the new literary magazine *The Rambler* found the opening performance of the first play undistinguished, but he very much liked the afterpiece, and he noted "Mrs. Poe's Tomboy gave surety of succeeding fame and favoritism."[9] As in Boston, it was Eliza who was off to a good start. No mention yet of David.

She now appeared twice as Cooper's leading lady, as Cora in *Pizarro* and as Ophelia in *Hamlet*. "Mrs. Poe is too light for Ophelia—" wrote *The Rambler's* critic, "she seemed wanting in sensibility in the earlier scenes, and the mad scene was robbed of most of its effect by a total exclusion of melancholy."[10] He continued, however, to admire her work as a comedienne, and he found her Morgiana in Richard B. Sheridan's and George Colman II's "grand operatical romance and spectacle" *The Forty Thieves* "very little, if anything, inferior to Mrs. Darley's,"[11] whom Eliza found herself following in New York just as she had in Boston.

The critic for *The Rambler* was a native American, "a young, plump, rosy-faced urchin,"[12] his editor David Longworth described him. There were few regular theatrical reviewers writing that season in New York, and in their absence, this young scribbler, as his contemporaries might have called him, was beginning to win a public through a series of articles he sent in to *The Rambler* under the title of the "Theatrical Register." His reviews sometimes contained such harsh criticism that even his editor eventually felt obliged to call them unfair, and unfortunately, David Poe became one of this critic's favorite targets.

It was in the beginning of the third week of the season that the rosy-faced urchin first began to take notice of David. He disliked almost entirely the company's performance of *Abaellino,* with Cooper in the title role and Eliza as his leading lady Rosamunda, and he found an inconsistency in the actors' pronunciation of one of the character's names, Dandoli. "The sage Falieri," he singled out David by the part he was playing, "would have it Dand-il-e. . . ."[13] It was this unfortunate slip of the tongue that gave *The Rambler's* critic the idea of nicknaming David "Dan Dilly" in his future reviews, all of which were to be unfavorable for David.

Meantime there were other reviews. An article in the *New York Evening Post* signed by Anglo Americus praised the company's production of Matthew G. Lewis's *Adelgitha,* saying it was as excellent as any seen in Convent Garden or Drury Lane. Eliza, again playing a young woman caught in a tragic conflict between her lover and her father, was Imma, a Byzantine princess. Though not the leading woman's role in the play, it was an excellent part, and the reviewer for the *New York Evening Post* praised her performance as "highly respectable . . . graceful and pleasing."[14] David was in the supporting role of Julian.

Eliza next played her first Desdemona to Cooper's Othello—in the then current altered version it is very nearly the same role as in Shakespeare's play. *The Rambler* disapproved. "Mrs. Poe is very unequal to Desdemona. It is much to be lamented that this lady should be thrust into parts for which she is so wholly unqualified."[15] The critic seems to have been determined to accept Eliza only as a comedienne, and he went on to say quite frankly that Mrs. Twaits was the only real tragedienne in the company, and since she was not attractive enough, the role should be filled by Mrs. Young. Later that season *The Rambler's* critic could be satisfied that his disapproval of Eliza as Desdemona had exerted some influence on the management. The next time Cooper played Othello, Mrs. Young was cast as his Desdemona. The management's susceptibility to his influence, however, could not have failed to have been an infuriating disappointment to Eliza. She was interested in becoming a complete actress, not only a comedienne, and if the managers were going to let a critic limit her to only one line of parts, her future at the Park was not promising.

On Wednesday, 27 September, during the fourth week of the season and on the playing night following Eliza's first performance as Desdemona, David, in an unexpected change in casting, was thrust at the last minute into the important part of the Spaniard Alonzo in *Pizarro.* He was replacing Hopkins Robertson, one of the Park's leading actors, who was out ill. David had played the smaller part of Daville in *Pizarro* earlier that season, but Alonzo was not a new role for him; he had played it in Boston during his and Eliza's appearances with John Howard Payne. *The Rambler* began its attack.

Mr. Poe was Mr. R.'s substitute in Alonzo; and a more wretched Alonzo have we never witnessed. This man was never destined for the high walks of the drama;—a footman is the extent of what he ought to attempt; and if by accident like that of this evening he is compelled to walk without his sphere, it would bespeak more of sense in him to read the part than attempt to act it;—his person, voice, and non-expression of countenance, all combine to stamp him—*poh! et praeterea nihil.*[16]

Ironically, David was faced with the identical situation that he had been his first season in Boston, except that this time the critic's personal insult had been directed at him rather than Eliza.

Not knowing who this anonymous writer was, David could not visit him personally as he had visited J. T. Buckingham in Boston; but the tone of *The Rambler's* later notices indicate that he must have had some kind of communication with the reviewer, either by a letter to the editor or even by a visit to the office of the magazine. Unfortunately, David had not learned from his experience with *The Polyanthos* how vulnerable such rebuttals made him. He was to find out.

As a kind of preamble to its "Theatrical Registry" for the next issue, *The Rambler* printed some crude lines in French using a word play on the similarity of the name Poe and the French word for pot, specifically chamber pot, and making clear that the reference was to David.[17] If the rosy-faced urchin's first attack on David was a personal insult, this latest was sheer abuse, and like any actor faced with this kind of publicity, David felt powerless to defend himself or his reputation, his own doubts and fears about his future as an actor being of little help in buoying his confidence or self-esteem.

Nor was the critic for *The Rambler* through with him yet. He continued to make David his favorite target, referring to him from now on only as "Dan Dilly." Of David's performance as Amos, a short but sharply etched cameo role of a misguided but loyal black slave in Elizabeth Inchbald's *To Marry or Not to Marry,* he wrote, "*Dan Dilly* played *Amos,* and in spite of the lampblack that covered his muffin face, there was no difficulty in penetrating the veil and discovering the worthy descendant of the illustrious Daniel." And in the same issue he added a note whose slant is so personal it suggests that David's communication either contained or implied a threat. In a day when men still fought duels this could have been a serious matter indeed, even for a rosy-faced urchin—or a reckless actor who was not a good shot.

By the by, it has been said, that this *gentleman* has taken some of our former remarks very much in dudgeon; but whether this be true or not, we entertain very great doubts, for certainly we have said nothing but the truth, and that should give no man offence. If it is the case, however, we are sincerely sorry for it; for from his amiable private character, and high *professional standing* he is among the last men we would justly offend. We own this to our friend Dan from having heard much of his spirit; for, for men of high spirit, we have a high respect, though no *fear.* This we beg to be explicitly understood; for as there are men who will sometimes mistake motives, it may happen that this conciliatory conduct on our part be imputed to causes foreign from the truth.[18]

Not satisfied with the hatchet job he had already done on David, *The Rambler's* young critic now chose to condemn him in a part that David had already played three times that season, "and was there anything else but Dan Dilly in the prince," he wrote of the fourth performance of the company's production of Thomas Dibdin's *Princess and No Princess,* "it would not be an uninteresting afterpiece. But poor *Dan* is fated to spoil whatever he undertakes, and like a millstone round the neck of a goose, he will be sure to drag it to the bottom in spite of all its buoyant properties."[19] And again in his final mention of David in his "Theatrical Registry," "Virolet in *The Mountaineers* was—but no matter—Dan Dilly played the part, and as far as the *gentleman* was concerned. . . ."[20]

Like so much of theatrical criticism, *The Rambler's* reviews of David's performances are much more a record of their author's own prejudices than they are a fair evaluation of David's work, and as such they reveal more of the critic than of the actor. Their effect on the young actor's life, however, was quite another thing. They could not have added to David's personal stability nor strengthened his professional standing, and all this was bound to affect Eliza.

Two writers did come to David's defense. In *The Rambler* itself David Longworth, the editor, published the following about his reviewer for the "Theatrical Registry": "our correspondant is too acrimonious; and I must take the liberty to differ from him in some measure, respecting Mr. Poe's talents, who, *if he would take pains,* is by no means contemptible."[21] Word of *The Rambler's* attack on David spread beyond New York, and there also appeared a letter in the Boston magazine *Something.*

To our brother Editors of New York
Gentlemen,
    We strongly and feelingly recommend to your encouragement and protection, the talents of Mr. Poe.—He *has* talents, and they may be improved or ruined by your just or incautious observations. We think, that the duty of an editor is first to feel, next to weigh, and lastly to determine.—We are well aware of the errors of this gentleman, but we know that such errors have frequently been introduced by unfeeling criticism. It is disgraceful in any editor to make actors on the stage a mere mark to shoot at.—If your intentions are to do good, encourage; if after you have done your duty, they do not improve—censure freely.

N. N.[22]

The initials of the writer of this letter are the same as those of the pen name of this magazine's editor, who signed his articles "Nemo Nobody," and historians believe that he was James Fennell.

After his performance as Virolet in *The Mountaineers* on 16 October, David appeared but once more at the Park Theatre. Two days later he played the featured role of Capt. Cypress in Richard Leigh's *Grieving's a Folly;* and although he was announced to appear again in this same role on Friday, 20 October, he did not. A short announcement in *The Rambler* noted a change in the bill owing to the "sudden insisposition of Mr. Robertson and Mr. Poe."[23] David's engagement at the Park had ended. It had lasted only six and a half weeks.

It is not known precisely why David left the company. He may have quit in mounting discouragement and frustration over his career. Stephen Price may have fired him—Price was a tough-minded businessman, and since David had already incurred his disfavor in the incident over the proposed concert earlier that year, Price could have found in David's bad notices a final reason to rid himself of a troublesome actor. The indisposition of which *The Rambler* speaks might also have been the beginning of an illness that made David unable to work. Some biographers believe that it was. Whatever the reason, David Poe's career as an actor had ended. His name no longer appears in the bills, and all traces of him vanish.

# The Park Theatre

DAVID'S CAREER had ended abruptly, but Eliza's continued to move ahead. At the Park Theatre she was playing some of the great tragic roles regularly. She would not achieve spectacular success in any of them, but she was only beginning in this line of parts. She was often appearing as a leading actress with Thomas Cooper, one of the foremost actors of her time. Eliza was barely twenty-two and by now had already been working as an actress for twelve years. She had still not yet become a mature artist nor had she achieved any great or brilliant success with either the critics or the public, but this was not unusual. At her age the great Sarah Siddons had played before the London public and also failed to make a strong impression.

Eliza had every reason to be happy with her professional life, but with her home life it must have been a very different story. The facts about David's whereabouts at this time are unknown. He may have still been with Eliza and their two sons Henry and Edgar, ages three and one, but if he were, Eliza was the breadwinner, and this would not have relaxed their already tense life together.

As always, however, in spite of her circumstances Eliza continued to work and to work hard. During the month following David's last appearance at the Park Theatre, she played frequently. She made her New York debut as Little Pickle, and audiences must have liked her in the part, for she eventually played it five times that season despite the lukewarm publicity of the reviews. Continuing in her repertoire from the afterpieces, she again appeared as Rosina, for which she received a mixed reception, *The Rambler* tersely describing her performance as "feeble,"[1] while the *Evening Post* was better: "In the afterpiece the charming voices of Mrs. Oldmixon and Mrs. Poe must have given pleasure to all the admirers of harmony."[2]

The company in which Eliza was working at the Park was a very strong one. Besides Cooper and Mrs. Oldmixon there were the well-known comedian William Twaits and his wife, the Charles Youngs, Joseph Tyler, Ann Storer Hogg, Hopkins Robertson, and Edmund Simpson. Mrs. Oldmixon, Joseph Tyler, and Ann Storer Hogg had long been well known in New York, ever since the days of the old American Company; and Edmund Simpson, who had just made a highly successful debut earlier in the season, was to have an enormously successful career at the Park, remaining there for thirty-eight years and eventually becoming co-manager with Stephen Price.

Again Eliza found herself associated with some of the finest actors in America, and as the season continued, she began to win more and more favorable notices in the press. Even the rosy-faced urchin began to become something of an admirer, and when she played Rosabelle in one of the company's biggest hits, William Dimond's *Foundling of the Forest*—a romantic and melodramatic spectacle, which drew long articles of praise in the *Evening Post* extolling its "elegant language" and "striking incidents"[3]—the redoubtable critic for *The Rambler* wrote of her performance, "Mrs. Poe was very clever in Rosabelle—there is a pertness and a volubility in her manner and delivery that is very appropriate."[4] But it was not until Eliza appeared as Cora in *Pizarro* and as Dolly Bull in John O'Keeffe's farce *John Bull at Fontainbleau* that *The Rambler*'s critic wrote his most fair-minded critiques of her work.

> We are always gratified with seeing Mrs. Poe on the stage; for as long as youth and sprightliness are attractive, she cannot fail to please. The part of Cora, however, is not exactly in that line in which she is calculated to shine. It was played with spirit and feeling, but wanted that softness and gentle tenderness which forms the distinguishing trait of the character. We point out the deficiency, because we think it possible that with a little attention she might infuse into her performance more of that softness so indispensably necessary to feminine grace and attraction; and further that we feel solicitous that she should attain that degree of excellence which, with a little exertion, we think is within her reach.
>
> In the afterpiece (*John Bull at Fontainbleau*) Mrs. Poe was excellent. It is in this line of characters she particularly delights and to which she should bend her chief attention. It is difficult to be sprightly without being fantastic, and to act the hoyden without being gross and mawkish. Mrs. Poe has hit the happy medium and let her cultivate it with assiduity. It is one of the most difficult and most important departments of female comedy.[5]

Playing these two roles on the same evening was the opportunity for Eliza to show the kind of versatility that an actress of her day prided herself in. A comedienne by instinct, she had gradually added a substantial number of serious parts to her repertoire during the last three seasons, and she had also achieved some important success in them.

On 16 January the theatre closed its doors for a winter break in its schedule. It was a needed break for Eliza, a time to rest, if possible, and gather up strength and courage to face what must have looked like a relentlessly demanding present and a very scary future. It also probably meant that she had no salary for five weeks.

The Park Theatre reopened on Washington's birthday, and shortly thereafter the management brought in John Howard Payne for five nights. Eliza again found herself cast as his leading lady. As she had in Boston, she played Cora, Ophelia, and Juliet with him, but unfortunately this time they did not share the great successes that they had had in Boston. The young Roscius's popularity was already beginning to wane, and while the *Evening Post* found his performances excellent, it lamented the lack of audience enthusiasm and response that had accompanied his first appearances at the Park.[6] For his benefit Payne played Zaphna in James Miller's translation of Voltaire's *Mahomet the Imposter,* and in this play Stephen Price cast Mrs. Twaits as his leading lady Palmyra. Eliza had played this role with Payne in Boston.

Price now brought in the prominent Drury Lane actor John Dwyer as his next attraction. A flamboyant performer and personality, Dwyer excelled in playing the airy, debonair gentlemen of the late eighteenth-century English comedies, his success in these roles, according to William Dunlap, never being "marred by his diffidence."[7] At first Eliza appeared in secondary parts with Dwyer, mostly in the soubrette line, but when his engagement was extended, and he added Mercutio to his repertoire, Eliza, in one of her most significant assignments at the Park Theatre, played Juliet. This was her second Juliet of that season and the third of her entire career. It would have been difficult anywhere in the country to bring together a finer company of actors than that with which she played Juliet at the Park that spring. The brilliant young actor Edward Simpson played Romeo, John Dwyer was Mercutio, and Mrs. Oldmixon played the Nurse.

The Park closed again toward the end of April for Easter Week, and when it reopened on 27 April, there were ten playing weeks left in the season. Eliza added a number of new roles to her repertoire during these closing weeks,[8] but it was not necessary to rehearse any of them under the furious pressures under which she had often been obliged to work in Boston. Her repertoire was now sufficiently large enough, and she no longer faced the enormous task of study that then confronted the apprentice actress. She now had at her fingertips a stock of parts of enormous scope and variety. In the last three seasons alone she had added over seventy roles to her repertoire.

In the meantime, Cooper, who had been away, returned to the company, and one of the first roles he played was Othello. Eliza had played Desdemona with him earlier in the season, but this time the managers cast Mrs. Young as Desdemona. Eliza again appeared as Cooper's Ophelia, and for the fourth time of the season she played Imma with him in Matthew G. Lewis's *Adelgitha.* When he played Lear, however, she was cast as Regan. This was a challenging departure from her usual line, but in the altered version Regan is not nearly so central a role as Cordelia, and two seasons previously in Boston, Eliza had played Cordelia to Cooper's Lear. By this time it was obvious that the management at the Park was unwilling to place Eliza before the public as a leading tragic actress, and this was probably one of the reasons that she agreed to take an engagement with Alexandre Placide and William Green, who had recently formed a partnership that played Charleston and the old Virginia Company circuit. She was to begin work shortly after the season at the Park closed.

During the actors' benefits, which began immediately after Cooper's final night, Eliza was thrown at the last minute into the role of Ellen Vortex in Thomas Morton's comedy, *A Cure for the Heartache*. There was scarcely time for rehearsal and not enough time for her to learn the lines. The *Columbian* reported that she nonetheless "gave much satisfaction."[9] Under such circumstances she was probably greatly relieved that she could read the part and did not have to depend too heavily on the Park's prompter and stage manager, Hibernian Oliff—whose promptings, according to William Dunlap, were all but unintelligible.[10]

On the performance night following her last-minute appearance as Ellen Vortex, Eliza played Rosa in the Park's extravagant production of Frederick Reynolds's "grand serio comic romance" *The Caravan*, a remarkable play set in Barcelona, in which one of the central characters is a Newfoundland dog. The play ends with an extraordinary scene in which the dog Carlo leaps from a rock into the river and is seen swimming after a drowning child, which he brings to the shore.[11] There is no record of how the Park managed all this, but the cues must have kept Hibernian Oliff busy.

For her own benefit, which was scheduled for the next-to-last performance night of the season, Eliza appeared as Rosamunda in William Dunlap's translation of *Abaellino* and as Narcissa in George Colman II's *Inkle and Yarico*. On the same day of her benefit performance two letters appeared in the *Columbian*.

> Mrs. Poe's benefit. The tragedy of *Abaellino*, and *Inkle and Yarico*, are advertised this evening for the benefit of Mrs. Poe. We hope that the public will not neglect this sprightly actress; her youth, appearance, and above all, her *private* misfortune, speak loudly in her favor. If she is not rewarded, then our pretensions to the appellation of a "generous public," are but slight indeed; for have we not by our neglect, tended to dampen the youthful ardor of Simpson, discourage the veteran abilities of Tyler, and rebuke the rare talents of Mrs. Oldmixon.
>
> Mercuito[12]

And this:

> Mr. Editor:
> From a consideration of duty to the well known merits of Mrs. Poe, the managers have benevolently bestowed that excellent and entertaining play of *Abaellino* for her benefit on the evening. It is to be hoped that a generous public will bestow on that worthy and respectable actress a crowded audience. The lovers of theatrical performance can never have an appeal in vain to their charitable dispositions when they recollect that Mrs. Poe stands in need of a respectable and full house. Let this be a stimulation to every exertion on their part to give aid to a female who has taken a benefit for the purpose of extricating herself from embarrassments occasioned by having two small

children to support out of the scanty pittance of her weekly wages. To those that are mothers, this appeal will really be unnecessary; as the calling of infants in distress will always bring to their aid a mother.

Let not the city of New York fall behind her sister states in fulfilling the expectation of this unbefriended female. Mrs. Poe's character stands far above mediocrity. Suffice it to say she is at once a respectable and an intelligent actress. Often she has drawn the shouts of applause from an enamored house by her superior address in the comic scene. It is a circumstance truly to be lamented, that New York is shortly to lose the entertaining actress, as she is shortly to embark for Charleston, to revive hilarity on their festive boards. Therefore let not this amiable woman experience any ingratitude from a neglect of the lovers of plays. Let us instill into her memory an everlasting remembrance of the bounty of New York when transported to another, but I trust not more generous place.

A friend to female merit[13]

The New Yorkers who read and responded to these appeals by attending Eliza's benefit that night all knew they would be helping her financially, but they did not all know the whole story. David had left her. She was now alone, the only support of her two small children, and during the last weeks of the season she had discovered that she was expecting her third child.

# 16

# "Oh! Sweet, Anna Page"

TWO WEEKS AFTER CLOSING in New York, Eliza joined the Placide-Green company in Petersburg, Virginia,[1] and she began rehearsals at the Back Street Theatre there knowing almost every actor in the company. Besides many of the regular members of the old Virginia Company with whom she had often appeared, the managers had also hired a number of actors who had been with her the preceding season at the Park Theatre. Her personal life may now in some ways have been a lonely one, but unlike Boston and New York she was not obliged to begin this engagement by working with strangers. The company closed this Petersburg season at the end of July and the actors all made the short trip north to Richmond.

Eliza had often come to Richmond at a turning point in her life: as a child after her mother's death, as Charles Hopkins's bride, and as his young widow. She had been in Richmond when she married David and they had decided to try their luck in the northern theatres; and now, coming back in August of 1810, she again faced a turning point.

Before her lay an uphill struggle for survival. She had always had two salaries to support herself and her children, but now there was only one. Henry was three, Edgar a little more than a year, and a third child was due in four months. It was a time when her responsibilities to her children and to her work probably occupied her every waking moment, leaving little time for her to think of herself. Nonetheless, it was the first time in her life she had ever been truly free to pursue her career independently. Her earliest work as an actress had all been under the guidance of her mother and then Thomas Wignell. As Charles Hopkins's wife she had been primarily known as the wife of a highly successful and precocious young actor. This had not been the case with David, but she had married him less than a year after Charles's death, and having her career strongly linked to David's had never been an advantage. Now, for the first time, she was completely on her own. Behind her was her first important success, and her reputation as an actress was steadily mounting. At twenty-three she had won the respect of her fellow workers and the praise and admiration of critics and audiences in every important theatre in the country. The experience and practice she had gained in having played over two hundred widely varied parts had by now given her a clear knowledge of her strengths and weaknesses as an actress. Her apprenticeship was nearing its end, and she was ready to being doing her most important work.

The company with which Eliza now began rehearsals for the Richmond opening was jointly managed by William Green and Alexandre Placide. The Virginia Company, as she had known it in earlier years, no longer existed. Indeed, only two months before she arrived back in Virginia, Margaret West had died in Norfolk, bringing the twenty years of the Wests' control of the Virginia circuit to an end.[2] The theatre in the South had always been very much a family affair, and it was in this tradition that the Placides had now succeeded the Wests.

This brilliantly talented family was headed by the flamboyant actor and acrobat Alexandre Placide, one of the most important figures in early American theatrical history. Eliza had known him most of her life, having first met him as a member of Sollee's company when she had played in Charleston in 1797 with her mother and step-father. The leading lady in Placide's company was his wife, the former Charlotte Wrighton. Their marriage had been accompanied with a great stir in conservative Charleston, since at the time Placide had kept a mistress who was generally thought to be his wife, but neither Charlotte's nor Alexandre's careers were affected by this scandal. They remained very popular performers, and they had a long marriage. Four of their six children, Caroline, Elizabeth, Jane, and Henry, followed their parents' profession and earned considerable reputations.[3]

Eliza had last rehearsed and played in the Richmond Theatre four years earlier when this ill-fated house had first opened its doors to the public. Now for the company's opening night on Saturday, 18 August, she played the heroine Angela in Matthew G. Lewis's fast moving thriller *The Castle Spectre.* The play takes place in a Gothic castle complete with sliding panels, secret doors, and gloomy subterraneous dungeon. There is even a spectacular ghost scene. In the afterpiece she was featured as Maria, the soubrette, in Thomas Dibdin's comic opera *Of Age Tomorrow.* Although these plays were considerably less substantial fare than she had been accustomed to playing in Boston and New York, Eliza was at least making her return engagement before the Richmond public in excellent roles.[4] Angela was rather new to her repertoire, but she had played Maria many times.

During the first five weeks of the season Placide and Green cast her primarily in roles from her standing repertoire as a comedienne and singer, and there were few new assignments. One of her most important new characters, however, was Letitia Hardy in Hannah Cowley's comedy *The Belle's Stratagem,* which she played for her benefit night during the fifth week of the Richmond engagement. It was a role well suited to her talents and an especially good choice for her benefit. She had excellent scenes and a song, and in the masquerade scene she danced a "double allemande" with Placide. This would have been a courtly, somewhat serious dance.

The play is a high comedy, and to succeed as Letitia, Eliza had to project the polished manners of a young and high-spirited lady brought up in the fashion-able London circles of the late eighteenth and the early nineteenth century. She had never been directly exposed to this kind of life—few Americans had—but she had worked with many actresses like Anne West, Mrs. Stanley, and Mrs. Oldmixon, who were expert at high comedy, and she had had ample opportunity to observe them. High comedy, or "genteel comedy," as Eliza's contemporaries often called this genre, was not entirely new to Eliza. From time to time she had appeared in Farquhar's, Vanbrugh's, and Sheridan's comedies, but always in secondary parts, because she had lacked the maturity for the leading roles. She was now ready to try them, and in doing so, was expanding her repertoire to include virtually every style of play then available to an actress.

Judging by the enthusiasm of this letter from the *Richmond Enquirer*, Eliza had enjoyed a great deal of success with the Richmond public in the five weeks before she played Letitia Hardy.

> From an actress who possesses so eminently the faculty of pleasing, whose powers are so general and whose exertions are so ready, it would be unjust to withhold the tribute of applause. Were I to say simply that she is a valuable acquisition to the Theatre, I should dishonor her merit and do injustice to the feelings of the public. . . . On the first moment of her entrance on the Richmond boards, she was saluted with the plaudits of admiration, and at no one moment since has her reputation sunk. Her "exits and entrances" equally operate their electric effects, for if we expect to be pleased when Mrs. Poe appears, when her part is ended, our admiration ever proclaims that our anticipations have been more then realized. It is needless to review the various characters in which her excellence has been displayed. I think I may be pardoned for asserting, that taking her performances from the commence-ment to the end, no one has acquitted himself with more distinguished honor. If it be the perfection of acting to conceal the actor, Mrs. Poe's name is a brilliant gem in the theatric crown. In a word, as no one has received more than she of the public applause, no one is better entitled to the public liberality.
>
> Were I to say more, Mr. Editor, perhaps I should forget the character I have assumed. In regard to Mrs. Poe, for a reason which the glass will tell her, it is a difficult thing to separate the *actress* from the *woman;* no wonder then, if it should be also difficult to separate the *critic* from the *man.* Even were Aristarchus himself to rise from the dead to sit in judgment on her acting he would find it necessary to put a strong curb upon his feelings. For if he did not, instead of criticising the *player,* he might find himself perhaps, in the situation of Shakespeare's Slender, dolefully heaving the lover's sigh and pathetically exclaiming, "Oh! sweet Anna Page."[5]

Eliza's beauty had always won her admirers, and when one studies the mini-ature of her dating from this period, it is easy to see why. The small portrait conveys a delicate beauty of feature—ivory skin tinged with a soft, talisman rose color at the cheeks and lips, a fine nose, tiny sensual mouth, and slightly dimpled, Cupid-like chin. The hair is light brown, fine, tightly curled, but not luxuriant. The artist has captured a warm, sweet, and sensitive expression in the eyes, which are light brown and project glowing vitality. There is a brilliance about this miniature, and it portrays a very proud and intelligent spirit.[6]

The company played in Richmond until early October, when it moved to Fredericksburg for a week's stand.[7] It returned to Richmond again the last week of October, the actors playing there for four more weeks, at the end of which John Dwyer, the Englishman with whom Eliza had played at the Park earlier that year, joined them for a week of guest performances before they moved down the James River to Norfolk.

Despite her pregnancy Eliza traveled on to Norfolk, and her time was very near when the company began its three-week engagement at the Fenchurch Street Theatre. Exactly how long she was able to play is unclear from the advertisements that survive.[8] She probably played Angela in *The Castle Spectre* and Maria in *Of Age Tomorrow* on the company's opening night, as she had done in Richmond, and she may also have appeared with John Dwyer, who had stayed on as guest performer with the company; but she could have done this only for a few performances. She had had to stop playing two weeks before the births of both Henry and Edgar, and she now probably did the same, leaving the repertory during the first or second week of the short Norfolk season. Not long after she gave birth to her third child, her first daughter, whom she named Rosalie.[9] Traditionally, the birth is given as 20 December, at the Forrest home, a Norfolk boarding house.

There were now three small children for Eliza to care for. Henry was five, Edgar was two, and Rosalie a small baby. There are accounts of a nurse in Norfolk with Eliza,[10] so that she must have had some help, but it was probably at this time, hard pressed by conflicting family and professional responsibilities, that she decided to send Henry to Baltimore to live with his grandparents. Surely it was a difficult decision to make, but under the circumstances it must have seemed the best, perhaps the only, thing to do.

When she had rested and was able to travel, Eliza went on to Charleston; within a little more than a month after Rosalie's birth she was back at work again.

It had been thirteen long years since she had last appeared on the stage of the Charleston Theatre. Ages ago, it must have seemed to her. Charlestonians could hardly have been expected to remember her as the eleven-year-old Miss Arnold who had appeared with the short-lived Charleston Comedians during the long ago spring of 1798, so the management billed her as Mrs. Poe "from the Boston, New York, and Philadelphia theatres," and reintroduced her to the Charleston public on the night of 23 January in the parts of Angela in *The Castle Spectre* and Priscilla Tomboy in *The Romp*. Her return to work had come more quickly than she had expected, because the bill originally announced for the 23d had to be canceled, and she had probably had hasty and last-minute rehearsals.[11] Fortunately, she had played both parts often and the company was virtually the same with which she had worked in Virginia. There had been some important changes since the Virginia engagement, however. William Twaits had succeeded Green as Placide's co-manager, and Matthew Sully, whom Eliza had known since she was a child, had joined the company in Charleston.

The Charleston Theatre was by now one of the older houses in the country. It had been built in 1793, another of the theatres that Thomas Wade West had built for the Virginia Company. Eliza had first played in it as a member of Sollee's company and then briefly during the same season with the Charleston Comedians. It stood on Broad and Middleton (New) Streets and had a "handsome pediment, stone ornaments, a large flight of stone steps, and a courtyard palisaded."[12] It was a large house with a fifty-six-foot circular front stage, designed somewhat like the Park Theatre's stage, and lit by three rows of patent or visible lamps. It contained three tiers of boxes, a pit, and a gallery, and it was brightly decorated with silver moldings and projections against a background of French white.

In the first seven weeks of the season[13] Eliza appeared frequently with John Dwyer, whose performances in Charleston were as successful as they had been in New York. During this time she was often his leading lady, playing some of the same roles she had played with him in New York, adding a number of new parts to her repertoire, and in two of the plays even taking on more difficult assignments than she had had in New York. Most important of all the new parts that she played with Dwyer, however, were her first attempts at two of the most famous roles in all of eighteenth-century repertory—Lydia Languish in *The Rivals* and Lady Teazle in *The School for Scandal.*

For Eliza, Lydia Languish was the culmination of the long line of sentimental heroines she had already played, and her thorough experience in impersonating these pallid and long-suffering ladies had given her an excellent background to understand the delicate satire with which Sheridan had drawn his heroine. Dwyer played her lover, Jack Absolute.

In playing Lady Teazle in Charleston, Eliza was following Mrs. Placide, "the Merry of the Virginia Theatres," who had played the part earlier that season. The company that the management brought together for *The School for Scandal* was an especially excellent one. William Twaits, in one of his best-known roles, was Sir Peter Teazle, Dwyer was Charles Surface, and Charles Young played Joseph Surface. In this, her first attempt at one of the truly great roles of English comedy, Eliza was again, as she had so often been in her career, in the best of company. She was also coming back to what was her forte, for it was as a comedienne that she had had her first successes; even as a child her instincts for comedy had been sure and strong. In a sense her apprenticeship had come full circle, except that now she could bring to her work a depth of experience that included the entire range of the repertoire available to an actress of her time.

Still a hard worker, she continued to learn new roles, and by mid-season she had played an extraordinarily wide variety of parts at the Charleston Theatre, from the elegant lady Eleanor of Elizabeth Inchbald's comedy *Every One Has His Fault* to the rustic farm girl Jane in John O'Keeffee's *Wild Oats*. Then there were her old friends Priscilla Tomboy, Little Pickle, Rosina, Molly Maybush, Caroline Dormer in *The Heir at Law,* Susan Ashfield in *Speed the Plow,* Melissa in Garrick's farce *The Lying Valet,* and Agnes in *The Mountaineers,* all of them characters that she had lived with for most of her life.

Along with her active schedule at the theatre, Eliza also found time to sing in two concerts,[14] one of them sponsored by the St. Cecilia Society, at the old Church Street Theatre, where she had last played with John Sollee's company. These concerts were strictly musical events and very elaborate affairs. Eliza sang on the programs with soloists on the flute, violin, pianoforte, and clarinet, playing works by the then contemporary composers Joseph Haydn, Rodolphe Kreutzer, Johann Cramer, and Ignaz Joseph Pleyel. Since music and dance were at that time so closely connected in the mind of the public, each concert was followed by a ball.

After the Easter layoff Eliza appeared as one of the leading performers in Matthew Sully's benefit.[15] She and Sully had known each other since they had first worked together in the Virginia Company as children. He was very well known in Charleston, and his benefit received excellent publicity. His little daughter appeared with him, carrying on the Sully tradition for the third generation.

For her benefit, on 29 April, three weeks before closing, Eliza played the leading role of Violante in Susannah Centlivre's *The Wonder.* This light-hearted comedy was then nearly a hundred years old. Set in Lisbon and centering on an extravagant and frivolous lovers' quarrel, the play demands very arch and skillful handling of many fanciful situations. In several of her scenes Eliza as Violante had to be very adept in the use of a fan and veil. Appearing as her jealous lover, Don Felix, a role that had been in Garrick's repertoire, was William Twaits. In the afterpiece Eliza played Moggy McGilpin for the first time that season, and Matthew Sully was Shelty, her leading man. She and Sully would have had vivid memories of the first night they had played these roles together. It had been in Norfolk during the summer of 1803, the night of the rowdy "theatrical fracas"[16] that the writer for the *Herald* had described so vividly. Charleston gave Eliza's benefit a good turnout, bringing her a much-needed and welcome profit that "answered her most sanguine expectations."[17]

The season ended on 20 May, and Eliza, accompanied by Edgar, Rosalie, and their nurse, set off with the company to Norfolk, where she planned to play for most of the summer.

# "One of Its Chief Ornaments"

THE WORKLOAD IN CHARLESTON had been very strenuous, and Eliza was exhausted. The physical and mental energy alone required in learning, rehearsing, and playing twenty-five new roles, as well as keeping up on those already in her repertoire, had been enough to push her endurance to the breaking point, but that had been only a part of the pressing demands made on her. There had also been the constant responsibility of her children. With feedings for her new baby it is doubtful that she had been able, even with a nurse, to sleep through the nights during a greater part of the Charleston season. She had moreover plunged abruptly into this taxing schedule only two weeks after Rosalie's birth, with no time to rest and regain her strength. With the constant drain on her energies day and night she could hardly have had time even to begin coming to terms with the failure and breakup of her marriage to David, and these unresolved frustrations would simply have worsened her depression. Without a proper rest, it was merely a question of when the inevitable breakdown would come.

And there was to be no rest during the summer, as there had been after the births of her other two children. The season at the Fenchurch Street Theatre opened only two and a half weeks after the company closed in Charleston, giving her just time to make the journey by sea from Charleston to Norfolk. She was to play in Norfolk until early August,[1] after which she was committed to an engagement in Richmond until the end of the year. Even if she had wanted a break from work, she probably could not have afforded it. With a nurse the household she was now supporting numbered four, and she was the only wage earner.

The hot summer season began in Norfolk with a number of changes in the company—including William Green, who had rejoined Alexandre Placide there as co-manager. Fortunately, there were no new assignments for Eliza. That was at least some relief; but she was not well, and for the first time there is evidence that her weakened condition was beginning to show in her appearance and in her work. On the day of her benefit the *Norfolk Herald* printed the following letter.

Sir, permit me to call the attention of the public to the benefit of Mrs. Poe and Miss Thomas for this evening. . . . The former of these ladies I remember (just as I was going in my teens) on her first appearance here met with the most unbounded applause—She was said to be one of the handsomest women in America; she was certainly the handsomest I had ever seen. She never came on the stage, but a general murmur ran through the house, "What an enchanting creature! Heavens what a form!—what an animated and expressive countenance!—and how well she performs! Her voice too! sure never any thing was half so sweet!"—Year after year did she continue to extort these involuntary bursts of rapture from the Norfolk audience, and to deserve them too; for never did one of her profession take more pains to please than she. But now "the scene is changed,"—Misfortunes have pressed heavy on her. Left alone, the only support of herself and several young children—Friendless and unprotected, she no longer commands that admiration and attention she formerly did. . . . And yet she is as assiduous to please as ever, and tho' grief may have stolen a few of the roses from her cheeks, still she retains the same sweetness of expression and symmetry of form and feature.[2]

A well-known actress's personal life is not her own, and Eliza, as she had in New York, once more saw her private misfortunes set down in the newspapers for all the world to see. This kind of appeal may have helped bring in audiences for her benefit, but how could she herself have read it without some embarrassment and distaste.

After the Norfolk closing Eliza, accompanied by Rosalie, Edgar, and their nurse, once more made the trip up the James River to Richmond, where she had spent a good part of her short life and where so much of significance had happened to her. She was well known there, and it was a city to which she must have felt a special attachment because of the many memories that it held for her. She was returning to it now at the lowest ebb of her life, and this is probably why the traditions that have robbed her of her true place in history took such strong root. It is true that she was in reduced circumstances when she arrived for her last engagement at the Richmond Theatre, but she was far from the unknown and poverty-stricken actress one often meets in the Poe biographies.

When the company played its opening week at the Richmond Theatre beginning on 14 August, Eliza did not appear frequently.[3] She may have been in *The Wonder* and *The Purse* on the opening night—she had played important roles in both these plays in Charleston—but later that same week she had to be replaced as Rosina, one of her most popular characters. The inescapable breakdown had begun. Her health was failing now, and although she did continue to work during the following six weeks and even learned a number of new roles, she was unable to carry a full load.

During the seventh week of the season she was given special billing as the maid Bridget in Charles Kemble's farce *A Budget of Blunders*. This was a new part, and the special billing may mean that she was attempting to return to more active performing; but if so, she was unsuccessful. Two weeks later, on her own benefit night, she was not announced for any major role.

On the performance night following this benefit she played Lady Santon, the Countess Wintersen, in Kotzebue's popular romantic melodrama *The Stranger.* Though not the leading part, Lady Santon is a pivotal role. The play ends with a tableau in which the heroine is reunited with her family and in which according to the playwright's directions "Lady Santon weeps, and every countenance sympathizes." It is with this vignette, so typical of the romantic plays with which Eliza Poe had spent most of her life, that the records of her career end.

The Richmond Theatre closed temporarily on 11 October, presumably for the company to play a short engagement in Fredericksburg or Petersburg during the races,[4] and when it reopened a week and a half later, Eliza was ill and out of the repertory.

It had been an exceptionally rainy and unhealthful summer throughout tidewater Virginia, and the hot and humid weather that often lasted into the early fall in the South had increased the danger of malaria, then known as "ague and fever."[5] It may have been malaria with which Eliza was stricken, as some biographers suggest, but her weakened physical condition following Rosalie's birth, aggravated by the gnawing anxieties and unrelenting pressures during the last year of her life, would have left her system dangerously unprotected against any virulent disease.

Whatever the precise disease she had contracted, Eliza fought it courageously. Four, five, six weeks she lay in a Richmond boarding house near the Washington Tavern on Ninth and Grace Streets where many of the actors were staying,[6] struggling to regain her strength and health. As her condition worsened with the passing weeks, and word of her reduced circumstances spread, she began to receive some help. She had played in Richmond since she was a child, and she had friends there. "A singular fashion prevails here this season," wrote the Richmond author Samuel Mordecai to his sister, "it is—charity. Mrs. Poe, who you know is a very handsome woman, happens to be very sick, and (having quarreled and parted with her husband) is destitute. The most fashionable place of resort, now is—her chamber—And the skill of cooks and nurses is exerted to procure her delicacies."[7] Among those who came to visit Eliza were Mrs. John Allan and Mrs. William MacKenzie, who took a special interest in Edgar's and Rosalie's welfare.

By the end of the seventh week of Eliza's illness, it was apparent that she was dying. On Friday, 29 November, her fellow actors gave her a special benefit, and above their advertisement in the *Virginia Patriot* they placed the following announcement:

### Mrs. Poe's Benefit

In consequence of the serious and long continued indisposition of Mrs. Poe, and in compliance with the advice and solicitation of many of the most respectable families, the managers have been induced to appropriate another night for her benefit—Taking into consideration the state of her health, and the probability of this being the last time she will ever receive the patronage of the public, the appropriation of another night for her assistance, will certainly be grateful to their feelings, as it will give them an opportunity to display their benevolent remembrance.[8]

The *Richmond Enquirer* also carried an appeal for the support of Eliza's benefit: "To the Humane Heart: On this night, Mrs. Poe, lingering on the bed of disease and surrounded by her children, asks your assistance; and asks it perhaps for the last time.—The generosity of a Richmond Audience can need no other appeal. For particulars, see the Bills of the Day."[9]

Eliza lived ten days beyond this benefit. She died Sunday morning, 8 December 1811, still a young woman, leaving three children, and abruptly ending a career that had scarcely begun. She was twenty-four years old. By the standards of the theatre in which she had grown up Eliza had only served an apprenticeship, but already she had gained a national reputation, and announcements of her death were carried not only in the Richmond papers, but in Boston and New York as well. "By the death of this lady," her obituary in the *Richmond Enquirer* read, "the stage has been deprived of one of its chief ornaments."[10]

On the Tuesday following her death Eliza's funeral procession assembled in the chilly morning air,[11] for it was now nearly winter, and at ten o'clock solemnly began its slow and steep way up Church Hill to St. John's Churchyard, where her body was laid to rest in a grave that would be unmarked for over a century.

# Epilogue
## "Her Brief Career of Genius and of Beauty"

NOT QUITE THREE WEEKS after Eliza's death, on the day after Christmas, a capacity crowd of over six hundred men, women, and children, "a gay and animated assembly"[1] including the newly elected governor of Virginia, George W. Smith, crowded into the Richmond Theatre for Alexandre Placide's benefit. During the second act of the pantomime, *The Bleeding Nun,* the orchestra had swung into full chorus and one of the actors had just made his entrance, when Hopkins Robertson stepped on the stage and to the horror of actors and public alike announced, "The house is on fire!" Sparks began falling on the stage, and Robertson ran to help some of the ladies from the boxes and onto the stage to escape through the stage door.

Within a short time the theatre was wrapped in flames and thick, sooty smoke. The audience panicked. Most of those in the pit were able to escape through the only door available to the audience. Those in the boxes were far less fortunate. They crammed into the narrow stairway leading to the exit; some threw themselves from the windows; some were trampled underfoot; some were even lifted over the heads of those pressing to escape. Many of them, including the governor, perished in the flames and smoke. Seventy-two died, many of their bodies charred so far beyond recognition that the site of the theatre was later declared a common grave for the victims.[2]

The city of Richmond went into mourning. An investigation revealed that the fire had started from an unextinguished wick in a chandelier used during one of the scenes and afterward drawn up into the flies. It first caught the scenery and then spread to the roof whose exposed rafters were covered by highly inflammable pine planks. Though to some of the pious the fire may have undoubtedly seemed a judgment from Heaven, the company was cleared of any blame or negligence by the investigating committee.

The only member of the acting company to die in the fire was the Greens' little daughter Nancy. All of the other actors escaped. In this they were fortunate, but they felt deeply the rift that the tragedy had put between them and the public. "We are conscious that many have too much cause to wish they had never known us," read their statement in the *Richmond Enquirer,* "we have lost our friends, our patrons, our property, and in part our homes." Their statement continued, "Never again shall we behold that feminine humanity which so eagerly displayed itself to soothe the victim of disease; and view with exaltation, the benevolent who fostered the fatherless, and shed a ray of comfort to the departed soul of a dying mother."[3] This is the last mention of Eliza Poe by her contemporaries, but it is not the end of her story.

She had left three children. Henry was in Baltimore with his grandparents. Edgar and Rosalie were with her in Richmond when she died. In Richmond, Rosalie was adopted by the William MacKenzies and Edgar was taken in, but not legally adopted, by the John Allans. If all of these arrangements were made before her death, Eliza died believing that her children would be provided for. Unfortunately, all of them were to lead profoundly troubled lives.

Henry spent most of his life in Baltimore. It is known that he visited Edgar in Richmond and that as a young man he went to sea. Some of his biographers believe that the writings he published under the intials "WHP" in the *North American Review* were in part collaborations with Edgar. In one of them he remembered leaving his mother.

For the North American

In a pocketbook I lately found three locks of hair, from which originated the following lines:—

> My Father's—I will bless it yet—
>   For thou hast given life to me:
> Tho' poor the boon—I'll ne'er forget
>   The filial love I owe to thee.
>
> My Mother's too!—then let me press
>   This gift of her I loved so well,—
> For I have had thy last caress,
>   And heard thy long, thy last farewell.
>
> My Rosa's! pain doth dim my eye,
>   When gazing on this pledge of thine—
> Thou wer't a dream—a falsity—
>   Alas! 'tis wrong to call thee mine!
>
> A Father! he hath loved indeed!
>   A mother! she hath blessed her son,—
> But Love is like the pois'ning weed,
>   That taints the air it lives upon.

W.H.P.[4]

At the time he wrote these lines, some fourteen years after he had gone to Baltimore, Henry's feelings about his sister had been deeply confused by a letter he had received from John Allan (the man who had become Edgar Poe's foster father) in which Allan stated that Rosalie was Henry's half sister.[5] Allan may have been in a position to know that Rosalie was not the daughter of the man whose name she bore throughout her lifetime, but he was a man of devious nature, and his motives for raising the question of Rosalie's legitimacy were probably personal. In this same extraordinary letter, for instance, he wooed Henry's favor by flattery, villified Edgar's character, asserted Rosalie's illegitimacy as if it were common knowledge, and finally ended his letter in a pious tone by praising his own charity to Edgar. Allan could have afforded some piety. He had two illegitimate children himself, and at the time he wrote the letter they were living in Richmond.[6] Nonetheless, the specter of Rosalie's illegitimacy raised by his letter has given rise to many theories as to whether David Poe was the father of Eliza's last child, but none of them are convincingly documented.

Henry died at twenty-four, at the same age as his mother. Toward the end of his short life, while they were living together in Baltimore, Edgar described him as "entirely given over to drink and unable to help himself."[7]

Rosalie, the youngest, was adopted by the William MacKenzies and lived mostly in Richmond. Though she lived longer than any of Eliza's children, she suffered from an arrested mental development, never growing to maturity. Despite the fact that Maria Clemm disliked her (and even once claimed she was not Eliza's daughter[8]), Rosalie kept contact with Edgar throughout his life, though she sometimes proved an embarrassment to him. As Edgar's legal heir she inherited many of his personal effects, some of which she sold. Rosalie ended her life in Washington at the Epiphany Church House, where she died at the age of sixty-three. She was buried there in a pauper's grave.

Eliza's most gifted son, Edgar, once remarked that he believed he "owed to his mother every good gift of his intellect or his heart,"[9] and indeed at the height of his fame his own recitals of his poetry, particularly "The Raven," greatly impressed his audiences and showed that the poet was the son of actors. To think that, had Eliza lived, Edgar, growing up in the theatre, would have been with people who valued his talents far more than his foster parents were ever capable of doing, is perhaps the most supremely ironic part of her story.

And what of David Poe? The tradition is that he was a "widower only two days"[10] and died shortly after Eliza, though there is no documentary evidence of either the date or the place of his death. Edgar Poe says that he died not more than two months after Eliza.[11] Maria Clemm says simply that he died of consumption at an early age.[12] Some biographers suggest that he died before Eliza, and it was even believed for a time that he died in Norfolk,[13] though none of the letters published for Eliza's benefits after her husband's disappearance in New York calls her a widow. "I was told," wrote Frederick W. Thomas about Henry Poe, whom he knew in Baltimore, in 1828, "by a lawyer intimate with the family that his father had deserted his mother in New York."[14] This is consistent with Samuel Mordecais' letter saying that Eliza and David had "quarreled and parted," especially since the letters appearing in the newspapers at Eliza's last

New York and Norfolk benefits describe her as being left alone rather than widowed. But beyond these scattered clues the facts surrounding the disappearance and death of David Poe are as unknown as those surrounding the last days in the life of his son Edgar, before the great poet was found ill and dying in a Baltimore hospital.

A hundred years after Eliza's death the Raven Society of the University of Virginia, where Edgar Poe had been a student, began a fund to locate her gravesite and erect a monument to her memory. It was not until 1928, however, when Actors Equity Association and the Edgar Allan Poe Shrine had joined the Raven Society in the undertaking, that a marker was finally erected. Poe's own words were chosen as the inscription:

> The actor of talent is poor at heart, indeed, if he do not look with contempt upon the mediocrity even of a king. The writer of this article is himself the son of an actress—has invariably made it his boast—and no earl was ever prouder of his earldom than he of the descent from a woman who, although well born, hesitated not to consecrate to the drama her brief career of genius and of beauty.[15]

# Chronology of Eliza Poe's Career and Repertoire

This chronology lists Eliza Poe's professional engagements as well as the nearly three hundred roles that she played during her lifetime. Both roles and engagements are only those that can be documented from contemporary newspapers that still exist—there were probably more. Generally, seasons run from September through August of the following year, but some overlapping has been inevitable. Pantomimes, in which Eliza appeared as dancer, singer, and actress are indicated by an asterisk.

FEDERAL STREET THEATRE, BOSTON, MASS.
Sang "The Market Lass" at her mother's benefit, 15 April 1796, her first appearance on the stage.

| Season | Character | Play | Author |
|---|---|---|---|
| 1796–97 | ASSEMBLY HALL, PORTSMOUTH, N.H. | | |
| July– | Maria | The Spoiled Child | Isaac Bickerstaffe |
| Nov. | Zorayda | The Mountaineers | George Colman II |
| | Bowman | Lethe | David Garrick |
| | Lucy | The Devil to Pay | Charles Coffey |
| | Phoebe | Rosina | William Shield |
| | Servant | The Apprentice | Arthur Murphy |
| | Gustava | Gustavas Vasa | Henry Brooke |
| | Biddy Belair | Miss in Her Teens | David Garrick |
| | Lavinia | The Fair Penitent | Nicholas Rowe |
| | Miss Nevill | She Stoops to Conquer | Oliver Goldsmith |
| | Polly | Polly Honeycombe | George Colman I |
| | Kate | The King and the Miller of Mansfield | Robert Dodsley |
| Nov.– | ASSEMBLY HALL, PORTLAND, MAINE | | |
| Jan. | Solomon Smack | Trick upon Trick | |
| | Little Pickle | The Spoiled Child | Isaac Bickerstaffe |
| Feb. | ASSEMBLY HALL, PORTSMOUTH, N.H. | | |
| | Letty | The Foundling | Edward Moore |
| | Prince Edward | Margaret of Anjou | George Colman II |

| Mar.–<br>Apr. | MARKET HALL, NEWPORT, R.I.<br>No new roles listed in advertisements. | | |

| Mar.–<br>Apr. | PROVIDENCE THEATRE, PROVIDENCE, R.I.<br>The Girl | *Children in the Wood* | Thomas Morton |

| Aug. | HARTFORD THEATRE, HARTFORD, CONN.<br>No new roles listed in advertisements. | | |

| Aug.–<br>Oct. | JOHN STREET THEATRE, NEW YORK, N.Y.<br>No new roles listed in advertisements. | | |

| 1797–98<br>Nov.–<br>Feb. | CITY THEATRE, CHARLESTON, S.C.<br>The Page<br>The Boy<br>Duke of York<br>Cupid<br>The Child<br>Dancing Nymph<br><br>Julia | *The Purse*<br>*The Adopted Child*<br>*Richard III*<br>*The Magic Chamber**<br>*Isabella*<br>*Americania and<br>   Eleutheria**<br>*The Sicilian Romance* | James Cross<br>Samuel Birch<br>William Shakespeare<br><br>Thomas Southerne<br><br><br>Henry Siddons |

| Mar. | THEATRE, WILMINGTON, N.C.<br>Norah | *The Poor Soldier* | John O'Keeffe |

| Apr.–<br>May | CHARLESTON THEATRE, CHARLESTON, S.C.<br>Nancy<br><br>Pink<br>Sophia | *Three Weeks after<br>   Marriage*<br>*The Young Quaker*<br>*The Road to Ruin* | Arthur Murphy<br><br>John O'Keeffe<br>Thomas Holcroft |

| 1798–99<br>Dec.–<br>Jan. | TEMPORARY THEATRE IN THE MARKET HALL, RICHMOND, VA.<br>Trusty | The Provoked<br>   Husband | John Vanbrugh |

| Feb.–<br>May | CHESTNUT STREET THEATRE, PHILADELPHIA, PA.<br>Poggie<br>Lauretta<br>Sicilian Girl<br>Moggy McGilpin | *Highland Festivity**<br>*False and True*<br>*Mysteries of the Castle*<br>*The Highland Reel* | Oscar Byrne<br>George Moultrie<br>Miles Peter Andrews<br>John O'Keeffe |

| | | |
|---|---|---|
| Fanny | *The Shipwreck* | S. James Arnold |
| Nina | *The Prisoner* | John Rose |
| Beda | *Bluebeard* | George Colman II |
| Nanette | *Blunders Repaired* | |

| May– | HOLLIDAY STREET THEATRE, BALTIMORE, MD. | | |
|---|---|---|
| June | Molly Maybush | *The Farmer* | John O'Keeffee |
| Oct.– | Principal Dancer | *The Constellation** | |
| Nov. | Prince John | *Henry IV, Part 1* | William Shakespeare |
| | Catalina | *The Castle of Andalusia* | John O'Keeffee |
| | Little Midshipman | *The Rival Soldiers* | John O'Keeffee |
| | Annette | *Robin Hood* | Leonard McNally |
| | Indian Woman | *Columbus* | Thomas Morton |
| | Singer | *Romeo and Juliet* | William Shakespeare |

| 1799– | CHESTNUT STREET THEATRE, PHILADELPHIA, PA. | | |
|---|---|---|
| 1800 | Dolly | *Lock and Key* | Prince Hoare |
| Dec.– | Maria | *The Sailor's Garland** | |
| May | Jane | *The Naval Pillar* | Thomas Dibdin |
| | Villager | *Fortune's Frolic* | John T. Allingham |
| | Belinda | *Modern Antiques* | John O'Keeffee |
| | Dancer | *Shelty's Frolic** | William Francis |
| | Priestess and Virgin of the Sun | *Pizarro* | August von Kotzebue/ Richard Sheridan (trans.) |
| | Penelope | *The Romp* | Isaac Bickerstaffe |
| | Genius | *The Grateful Lion** | |
| | Chorus | *Macbeth* | William Shakespeare |

| May– | HOLLIDAY STREET THEATRE, BALTIMORE, MD. | | |
|---|---|---|
| June | Irish Lilt | *Shelty's Frolic** | William Francis |
| | Ellen | *Sighs* | August von Kotzebue/ Prince Hoare (trans.) |
| | Nancy | *The Naval Pillar* | Thomas Dibdin |
| | Cornelia | *The Positive Man* | John O'Keeffee |

| Aug.– | U.S. THEATRE IN THE LOTTERY HOTEL, WASHINGTON, D.C. | | |
|---|---|---|
| Sept. | Wilelmina | *The Waterman* | Charles Dibdin |
| | Dancer | *Romeo and Juliet* | William Shakespeare |
| | Priscilla Tomboy | *The Romp* | Isaac Bickerstaffe |

| 1800– | CHESTNUT STREET THEATRE, PHILADELPHIA, PA. | | |
|---|---|---|---|
| 1801 | Irene | *Bluebeard* | George Colman II |
| Oct.– | Welsh Girl | *St. David's Day* * | |
| Apr. | Cupid | *Cymon and Sylvia* | David Garrick |
| | Celia | *A Trip to Fontainbleau* | John O'Keeffee |
| | Catherine | *Netley Abbey* | William Pearce |
| | Nelly | *No Song, No Supper* | Prince Hoare |
| | Lass | *Christmas Gambols* * | |
| | Prince of Wales | *Richard III* | William Shakespeare |
| | Agnes | *The Follies of a Day* | Thomas Holcroft |
| | Nancy | *The Shakespeare Jubilee* | David Garrick |
| | Rosina | *The Corsicans* | August von Kotzebue |
| | Dancer | *Aladdin* * | |
| | Dancer | *Management* | Frederick Reynolds |
| | Singer | *Isabella* | Thomas Southerne |
| | Singer | *The Castle Spectre* | August von Kotzebue |
| | Attendant | *The Law of Lombardy* | Robert Jephson |
| | Country Lass | *Speed the Plow* | Thomas Morton |
| | Singer | *Alexander the Great* * | Nathaniel Lee |
| | Zilia | *Peru Revenged* | Frederick Reynolds |
| | Singer | *Point of Honor* | John Phillip Kemble |

| Apr.– | HOLLIDAY STREET THEATRE, BALTIMORE, MD. | | |
|---|---|---|---|
| June | Laura | *Lock and Key* | Prince Hoare |
| | Ghita | *The Siege of Belgrade* | William Cobb |
| | Girl | *The Count of Burgundy* | August von Kotzebue |
| | Visiting Lady | *The Deaf Lover* | Frederic Pilon |
| | Principal singer | *Virgin of the Sun* | August von Kotzebue/ Richard Sheridan (trans.) |
| | Dancer | *The Merchant of Venice* | William Shakespeare |

| July | SOUTHWARK THEATRE, PHILADELPHIA, PA. | | |
|---|---|---|---|
| | Ophelia | *Hamlet* | William Shakespeare |

| 1801–2 | CHESTNUT STREET THEATRE, PHILADELPHIA, PA. | | |
|---|---|---|---|
| Dec.– | Camira | *Il Bondocani* | Thomas Dibdin |
| Apr. | Grace Gaylove | *The Review* | George Colman II |
| | Fanny Liberal | *School for Prejudice* | Thomas Dibdin |

|          | Sam's Wife | *Obi, or Three Fingered Jack* * |                    |
|          | First Actress | *The Manager in Distress* | George Colman II |
|          | Dancer | *The Scheming Milliner* * | William Francis |
|          | Attendant Nymph | *Hercules and Omphale* * |                    |

| Apr.– June | HOLLIDAY STREET THEATRE, BALTIMORE, MD. |  |  |
|------------|------|------|------|
|          | Juba | *The Prize* | Prince Hoare |
|          | Mary | *The Turnpike Gate* | Thomas Knight |
|          | Angelica | *The Shipwreck* | S. James Arnold |
|          | Fatima | *Bluebeard* | George Colman II |
|          | Eugene | *Joanna of Montfaucon* | August von Kotzebue |
|          | Sukey Starch | *Harlequin Hurry Scurry* * |  |
|          | Attendant | *The Mourning Bride* | William Congreve |
|          | Diana | *The London Hermit* | John O'Keeffee |
|          | Lass | *The Sailor's Landlady* |  |
|          | Attendant | *The Earl of Essex* |  |
|          | Singer | *Alexander the Great* * | Nathaniel Lee |
|          | Nancy/Miranda | *The Shakespeare Jubilee* | David Garrick |
|          | Country Girl | *Lover's Vows* | John Vanbrugh |
|          | Circassian | *The Corsair* * |  |
|          | Herman | *Adelmorn the Outlaw* | Matthew G. Lewis |

July      SOUTHWARK THEATRE, PHILADELPHIA, PA.
          No new roles listed in advertisements.


1802–3    LIBERTY HALL, ALEXANDRIA, VA.
Aug.–     No new roles listed in advertisements.
  Sept.


Sept.–    FREDERICKSBURG THEATRE, FREDERICKSBURG, VA.
  Oct.    No new roles listed in advertisements.

Nov.–     BACK STREET THEATRE, PETERSBURG, VA.
  Dec.

|          | Charlotte | *English Readings* | James Cobb |
|          | Louisa | *No Song, No Supper* | Prince Hoare |
|          | Zelina | *Oberon* | John Daly Burk |

| Dec.– | TEMPORARY THEATRE IN THE MARKET HALL, RICHMOND, VA. | | |
|---|---|---|---|
| Jan. | No new roles listed in advertisements. | | |

| Mar.– | FENCHURCH STREET THEATRE, NORFOLK, VA. | | |
|---|---|---|---|
| May | Louisa | *Sighs* | August von Kotzebue |
| | Mary Tactic | *The Rival Soldiers* | John O'Keeffe |
| | Elmira | *The Sultan* | Isaac Bickerstaffe |
| | Miss Nancy | *Fortune's Frolic* | John Till Allingham |
| | Jenny | *The Fruitless Precaution** | |
| | Eliza | *The Flitch of Bacon* | Henry Bate |
| | Orilla | *Adelmorn the Outlaw* | Matthew G. Lewis |
| | Rose Sydney | *Secrets Worth Knowing* | Thomas Morton |

| May | BACK STREET THEATRE, PETERSBURG, VA. | | |
|---|---|---|---|
| | Floretta | *May Day Dower** | |

| June– | FENCHURCH STREET THEATRE, NORFOLK, VA. | | |
|---|---|---|---|
| July | Adelaide | *Prisoner at Large* | John O'Keeffe |

| 1803–4 | LIBERTY HALL, ALEXANDRIA, VA. | | |
|---|---|---|---|
| Aug.– | Lydia | *The Sixty-Third Letter* | Wally C. Oulton |
| Sept. | Emily | *The Jew and the Doctor* | Thomas Dibdin |

| Sept.– | FREDERICKSBURG THEATRE, FREDERICKSBURG, VA. | | |
|---|---|---|---|
| Oct. | No new roles listed in advertisements. | | |

| Nov. | BACK STREET THEATRE, PETERSBURG VA. | | |
|---|---|---|---|
| | Maria | *The School for Scandal* | Richard B. Sheridan |

| Dec.– | QUARRIER'S TEMPORARY THEATRE, RICHMOND, VA. | | |
|---|---|---|---|
| Apr. | No new roles listed in advertisements. | | |

| Apr.– | BACK STREET THEATRE, PETERSBURG, VA. | | |
|---|---|---|---|
| June | Floranthe | *The Mountaineers* | George Colman II |

| July– | QUARRIER'S TEMPORARY THEATRE, RICHMOND, VA. | | |
|---|---|---|---|
| Sept. | Susan | *Speed the Plow* | Thomas Morton |
| | Caroline | *The Heir at Law* | George Colman II |
| | Mrs. Malford | *The Soldier's Daughter* | Adam Cherry |
| | Stella | *The Maid of Bristol* | James Boaden |
| | Julio | *Deaf and Dumb** | |

| 1804–5 Sept.– Oct. | FREDERICKSBURG THEATRE, FREDERICKSBURG, VA. No new roles listed in advertisements. | | |
|---|---|---|---|

| Oct.– Nov. | BACK STREET THEATRE, PETERSBURG, VA. No new roles listed in advertisements. | | |
|---|---|---|---|

| Dec.– Mar. | QUARRIER'S TEMPORARY THEATRE, RICHMOND, VA. | | |
|---|---|---|---|
| | Narcissa | *Inkle and Yarico* | George Colman II |
| | Peggy Plainway | *Raising the Wind* | James Kenney |
| | Mary Thornberry | *John Bull* | George Colman II |
| | Emily | *The Poor Gentleman* | George Colman II |
| | Clara | *The Adopted Child* | Samuel Birch |
| | Honoria | *Notoriety* | Frederick Reynolds |
| | Melissa | *The Lying Valet* | David Garrick |

| Mar– July | FENCHURCH STREET THEATRE, NORFOLK, VA. | | |
|---|---|---|---|
| | Lenora | *Like Master, Like Man* | Thomas Ryder |

| 1805–6 Sept.– Oct. | WASHINGTON THEATRE, WASHINGTON, D.C. | | |
|---|---|---|---|
| | Kitty | *Ways and Means* | George Colman II |

| Oct. | FREDERICKSBURG THEATRE, FREDERICKSBURG, VA. No new roles listed in advertisements. | | |
|---|---|---|---|

| Oct.– Dec. | WASHINGTON THEATRE, WASHINGTON, D.C. No new roles listed in advertisements. | | |
|---|---|---|---|

| Jan.– May | RICHMOND THEATRE, RICHMOND, VA. | | |
|---|---|---|---|
| | Anna | *Douglas* | John Home |
| | Charlotte | *The Gamester* | Edward Moore |
| | Julia | *The Sailor's Daughter* | Richard Cumberland |
| | Amy | *Who Wants a Guinea* | George Colman II |
| | Sophia | *The Blind Bargain* | Frederick Reynolds |
| | Julia | *The Midnight Hour* | Elizabeth Inchbald |
| | Lady Randolph | *Douglas* | John Home |
| | Miss Juvenile | *A New Way to Win Hearts* | |
| | Harriet Manly | *The Will for the Deed* | Thomas Dibdin |

| Apr. | BACK STREET THREATRE, PETERSBURG, VA. | | |
|---|---|---|---|
| | Zamora | *The Honeymoon* | John Tobin |

| June– | CHESTNUT STREET THEATRE, PHILADELPHIA, PA. | | |
|---|---|---|---|
| July | Agnes | *The Mountaineers* | George Colman II |
| | Kitty Sprightly | *All the World's a Stage* | Isaac Jackman |

| July | VAUXHALL GARDENS SUMMER THEATRE, NEW YORK, N.Y. |
|---|---|
| | No new roles listed in advertisements. |

| 1806–7 | FEDERAL STREET THEATRE, BOSTON, MASS. | | |
|---|---|---|---|
| Oct.– | Miss Blandford | *Speed the Plow* | Thomas Morton |
| May | Amelia | *Lovers Vows* | Elizabeth Inchbald |
| | Gillian | *The Quaker* | Charles Dibdin |
| | Jessy Oatland | *A Cure for the Heartache* | Thomas Morton |
| | Virginia | *Paul and Virginia* | James Cobb |
| | Leonora | *The Padlock* | Isaac Bickerstaffe |
| | Fanny | *The Clandestine Marriage* | David Garrick and George Colman I |
| | Mary | *The Maid of the Oaks* | John Burgoyne |
| | Barbara | *The Iron Chest* | George Colman II |
| | Margaretta | *No Song, No Supper* | John O'Keeffe |
| | Miss Jenny | *The Provoked Husband* | John Vanbrugh |
| | Laura | *Five Miles Off* | Thomas Dibdin |
| | Princess Lodoiska | *Lodoiska* | John Philip Kemble |
| | Marianna | *The Miser* | Henry Fielding |
| | Clorinda | *Robin Hood* | Leonard McNally |
| | Sophy | *Which Is the Man?* | Hannah Cowley |
| | Cherry | *The Beaux Stratagem* | George Farquhar |
| | Cordelia | *King Lear* | William Shakespeare |
| | Blanch | *King John* | William Shakespeare |
| | Fidelia | *The Foundling* | Edward Moore |
| | Cora | *Columbus* | Thomas Morton |
| | Volante | *The Honeymoon* | John Tobin |
| | Olivia | *The Delinquent* | Frederick Reynolds |
| | Italian Girl | *The Critic* | Richard B. Sheridan |
| | Lydia | *Love Laughs at Locksmiths* | George Colman II |

| | | |
|---|---|---|
| Cora | *Pizarro* | August von Kotzebue/ Richard B. Sheridan (trans.) |
| Sophia | *The Lie of a Day* | John O'Keeffe |
| Cymon | *Cymon and Sylvia* | David Garrick |
| Laura | *The Agreeable Surprize* | John O'Keeffe |
| Ariel | *The Tempest* | William Shakespeare |
| Betsey Blossom | *The Deaf Lover* | Frederick Pilon |
| Sally Williams | *Glory of Columbia* | William Dunlap |
| Fanny | *The Mogul Tale* | Elizabeth Inchbald |
| Rosamunda | *Abaellino* | Heinrich Zschokke/ William Dunlap (tr.) |
| Dollalolla | *The Tragedy of Tragedies* | Henry Fielding |
| Josephine | *Children in the Wood* | Thomas Morton |

| | | | |
|---|---|---|---|
| 1807–8 | | FEDERAL STREET THEATRE, BOSTON, MASS. | |
| Sept.– | Donna Clara | *The Duenna* | Richard B. Sheridan |
| Apr. | Witch | *Macbeth* | William Shakespeare |
| | Rosalie | *Town and Country* | Thomas Morton |
| | Genevieve | *The Hunter of the Alps* | William Dimond |
| | Jessica | *The Merchant of Venice* | William Shakespeare |
| | Variella | *The Weathercock* | John Till Allingham |
| | Venus | *Cinderella** | |
| | Cicely | *The Heir at Law* | George Colman II |
| | Phoebe | *Wags of Windsor* | George Colman II |
| | Maria | *Of Age Tomorrow* | Thomas Dibdin |
| | Albina | *The Will* | Frederick Reynolds |
| | Arabella | *More Ways than One* | Hannah Cowley |
| | Cora | *The Virgin of the Sun* | August von Korzebue/ Frederick Reynolds (trans.) |
| | Selina | *A Tale of Mystery* | Thomas Holcroft |
| | Louisa | *The Sailor's Daughter* | Richard Cumberland |
| | Pleasure | *Harlequin's Choice** | |
| | Zelidy | *Time's a Tell Tale* | Henry Siddons |
| | Ellen | *The Wise Men of the East* | August von Kotzebue/ |

|  |  |  | Elizabeth Inchbald (trans.) |
|--|--|--|--|
|  | Amelia | *The Robbers* | Friedrich Schiller/ John Hodgkinson (trans.) |
|  | Ella | *Ella Rosenberg* | James Kenney |

| June and Aug. | BACK STREET THEATRE, PETERSBURG, VA. | | |
|--|--|--|--|
|  | Irene | *Barbarossa* | John Brown |

| 1808–9 Sept.– Apr. | FEDERAL STREET THEATRE, BOSTON, MASS. | | |
|--|--|--|--|
|  | Emily | *False Alarms* | James Kenney |
|  | Antonia | *Two Faces under a Hood* | Thomas Dibdin |
|  | Charlotte | *The Apprentice* | Arthur Murphy |
|  | Marcella | *A Bold Stroke for a Husband* | Hannah Cowley |
|  | Christina | *Gustavas Vasa* | Henry Brooke |
|  | Rachael | *Feudal Times* | George Colman II |
|  | Emma | *We Fly by Night* | George Colman II |
|  | Palmyra | *Mahomet* | James Miller |
|  | Juliet | *Romeo and Juliet* | William Shakespeare |
|  | Sigismunda | *Tancred and Sigismunda* | James Thomson |
|  | Abdalla | *Il Bondacani* | Thomas Dibdin |
|  | Serina | *The Black Castle* | J. H. Amherst |
|  | Marianna | *Lindor and Clara* | James Fennell |
|  | Miss Marchmont | *False Delicacy* | Hugh Kelly |

| 1809–10 Sept.– July | PARK THEATRE, NEW YORK, NY. | | |
|--|--|--|--|
|  | Angela | *The Castle Spectre* | Matthew G. Lewis |
|  | Morgiana | *The Forty Thieves* | Richard B. Sheridan and George Colman II |
|  | Imma | *Adelgitha* | Matthew G. Lewis |
|  | Desdemona | *Othello* | William Shakespeare |
|  | Elisena | *Princess and No Princess* | Thomas John Dibdin |
|  | Bertha | *The Point of Honor* | John Philip Kemble |
|  | Dorcas | *The Mock Doctor* | Molière/ |

| | | Henry Fielding (trans.) |
|---|---|---|
| Parisatis | *Alexander the Great* | Nathaniel Lee |
| Judith | *The Young Quaker* | John O'Keeffee |
| Rosabelle | *The Foundling of the Forest* | William Dimond |
| Teresa | *Venoni* | Matthew G. Lewis |
| Dolly Bull | John Bull at Fontainbleau | John O'Keeffee |
| Miss Ogle | *The Belle's Stratagem* | Hannah Cowley |
| Lucy | *George Barnwell* | George Lillo |
| Fisherwoman | *Don Juan\** | |
| Widow Bellair | *The Widow or Who Wins* | John Till Allingham |
| Dorothy | *Laugh When You Can* | Frederick Reynolds |
| Miss Godfrey | *The Lyar* | Samuel Foote |
| Lucetta | *The Suspicious Husband* | Benjamin Hoadley |
| Leonora | *Two Strings to Your Bow* | Robert Jephson |
| Catharine | *The Exile* | Frederick Reynolds |
| Eliza | *Riches or the City Madam* | James Bland Burges |
| Emily | *Not at Home* | R. C. Dallas |
| Valeria | *Coriolanus* | William Shakespeare |
| Regan | *King Lear* | William Shakespeare |
| Ruth | *The Honest Thieves* | Thomas Knight |
| Taffline | *Town and Country* | Thomas Morton |
| Ulrica | *The Free Knights* | Frederick Reynolds |
| Edward | *Everyone Has His Fault* | Elizabeth Inchbald |
| Rosa | *The Caravan* | Frederick Reynolds |

July — BACK STREET THEATRE, PETERSBURG, VA.

| | | |
|---|---|---|
| Miss Doiley | *Who's the Dupe* | Hannah Cowley |
| Mrs. Changeable | *The Jew and the Doctor* | Thomas Dibdin |

Aug.–Sept. — RICHMOND THEATRE, RICHMOND, VA.

| | | |
|---|---|---|
| Florence | *The Curfew* | John Tobin |
| Emily | *The Battle of Eutaw Springs* | William Joor |
| Letitia | *The Belle's Stratagem* | Hannah Cowley |

| | | |
|---|---|---|
| 1810–11 | FREDERICKSBURG THEATRE, FREDERICKSBURG, VA. | |
| Oct. | No new roles listed in advertisements. | |
| Oct.–Nov. | RICHMOND THEATRE, RICHMOND, VA. No new roles listed in advertisements. | |
| Nov.–Jan. | FENCHURCH STREET THEATRE, NORFOLK, VA. No new roles listed in advertisements. | |
| Jan.–May | CHARLESTON THEATRE, CHARLESTON, S.C. | |
| | Jacintha | *The Suspicious Husband* | Benjamin Hoadley |
| | Louisa | *The Dramatist* | Frederick Reynolds |
| | Lydia Languish | *The Rivals* | Richard B. Sheridan |
| | Lady Eleanor | *Every One Has His Fault* | Elizabeth Inchbald |
| | Louisa | *The Irishman in London* | William Macready |
| | Lady Teazle | *The School for Scandal* | Richard B. Sheridan |
| | Jane | *Wild Oats* | John O'Keeffe |
| | Miss Grantam | *The Lyar* | Samuel Foote |
| | Dimity | *Three Weeks after Marriage* | Arthur Murphy |
| | Ismena | *The Sultan* | Isaac Bickerstaffe |
| | Fiorella | *My Grandmother* | Prince Hoare |
| | Christine | *Tekeli* | Theodore Edward Hook |
| | Margaretta | *No Song, No Supper* | Prince Hoare |
| | Flora | *The Midnight Hour* | Elizabeth Inchbald |
| | Dolly | *Hit or Miss* | Isaac Pocock |
| | Donna Clara | *Two Strings to Your Bow* | Robert Jephson |
| | Francisca | *Don Juan** | |
| | Sally | *The Purse* | James Cross |
| | Violante | *The Wonder* | Susannah Centlivre |
| | Fanny | *Man and Wife* | Samuel J. Arnold |
| | Nancy Joblin | *The Poor Lodger* | W. C. White |
| | Albina | *The Grandfather's Will* | |
| | Nancy | *Blackbeard the Pirate** | |
| | Almeida | *Blackbeard the Pirate** | |
| | Lucy | *The Review* | George Colman II |

| June–<br>Aug. | FENCHURCH STREET THEATRE, NORFOLK, VA.<br>No new roles listed in advertisements. | | |
|---|---|---|---|
| Aug.–<br>Nov. | RICHMOND THEATRE, RICHMOND, VA. | | |
| | Bridget | *Budget of Blunders* | Charles Kemble |
| | Lady Santon | *The Stranger* | August von<br>Kotzebue/<br>Richard B. Sheridan<br>(trans.) |

# Notes

## Preface

1. The use of the name Eliza in this biography requires explanation. The *New York Evening Post*, 12 December 1811, gives this obituary for Mrs. Poe: "Died, at Richmond on the 7th of December, Mrs. Eliza Poe, formerly of the N.Y. Theatre." The marriage bond with David Poe, dated 14 March 1806, calls her "Mrs. Eliza Hopkins, widow of Charles D. Hopkins, dec'd. of the City of Richmond." These are the documents upon which I base my belief that Poe's mother was known as Eliza. A facsimile of the marriage bond appears in Arthur Hobson Quinn's *Edgar Allan Poe* (New York and London: D. Appleton-Century Co., Inc.), p. 23. I do not know why Quinn himself did not use the name Eliza unless he was unaware of the New York obituary or unless he thought the name on the marriage bond was either an abbreviation or a mistake. The name Elizabeth was first used by John Ingram, and all of Poe's biographers have since used it. None of them cites any documentary evidence for the name. It is important to remember that Ingram gathered his information about Eliza through his correspondence with contemporaries, acquaintances, and relatives of Poe more than fifty years after Eliza's death. Few of them knew her at all, and none of them knew her well. Susan Archer Weiss used the name Betty in *The Home Life of Poe* (New York: The Broadway Publishing Co., 1907) and both Mary E. Phillips and Frances Winwar did the same. Quinn, however, shows *The Home Life of Poe* (Quinn, pp. 730–41) to be an unreliable source. It is my belief that the documents I cite, the marriage bond and the obituary, are the most valid sources available for accurately determining Mrs. Poe's first name.

## Chapter 1. "The Market Lass"

1. *Boston Massachusetts Mercury*, 5 January 1796.

2. Ibid.

3. *Boston Centinel*, 6 January 1796; *Boston Massachusetts Mercury*, 5 January 1796.

4. John Bernard, *Retrospections of America, 1797–1811* (New York: Harper & Bros., 1887), p. 263.

5. For the general historical information including the incident in founding the Boston Theatre, see William Dunlap, *A History of the American Theatre* (New York: J. & J. Harper, 1832), and George O. Seilhamer, *A History of the Theatre* (Philadelphia: Globe Printing House, 1888–91).

6. Bernard, *Retrospections*, p. 29.

7. *Boston Centinel*, 9 April 1796.

8. For descriptions of the Federal Street Theatre, see John Alden, "A Season in Federal Street," *Proceedings of the American Antiquarian Society*, April 1955 (Worcester, Mass.: American Antiquarian Society, 1955), pp. 11–12; Mary Carolina Crawford,

*Romance of the American Theatre* (Boston: Little Brown and Company, 1913), pp. 114–15; and Brooks McNamara, *The American Playhouse in the Eighteenth Century* (Cambridge: Harvard University Press, 1969), pp. 122–25.

9. For details of the Boston season during the spring of 1796, see William W. Clapp, *A Record of the Boston Stage* (Boston: J. Munroe, 1853), pp. 34–39, and Seilhamer, *History of the Theatre*: 297–313.

10. Alden, "A Season in Federal Street," pp. 32–36.

11. Ibid., p. 19; see also note 20 quoting manuscript agreement between C. S. Powell and his trustees dated 7 January 1794 in the Boston Public Library, Allen A. Brown Collection.

12. The fines are listed in "Rules and Regulations," MsTh 4 (11), from the Brown Collection in the Boston Public Library.

13. *Boston Massachusetts Mercury*, 16 February 1796.

14. Bernard, *Retrospections*, p. 263.

### Chapter 2. "A Miss of Only Nine Years Old"

1. *Boston Centinel*, 21 May 1796; *Boston Massachusetts Mercury*, 31 May 1796.

2. James Moreland, "The Theatre in Portland in the 18th Century," *New England Quarterly* 11 (June 1938): 332.

3. Bernard, *Retrospections*, pp. 318, 319.

4. Seymour Dunbar, *A History of Travel in America* (New York: Tudor Publishing Co., 1937), p. 742.

5. For details about the first Portsmouth season including other performers in Portsmouth, see the ads appearing in the *Portsmouth New Hampshire Gazette* and *Portsmouth Oracle of the Day* from 21 July to 9 November 1796.

6. John Durang, *The Memoir of John Durang*, ed. Alan S. Downer (Pittsburgh: University of Pittsburgh Press, 1966), p. 69.

7. Yvonne Ffrench, *Mrs. Siddons* (London: Derek Verschoyle, 1936), p. 11.

8. *Portsmouth Oracle of the Day*, 2 November 1796.

9. In all subsequent advertisements Eliza's mother is billed as "Mrs. Tubbs."

10. *Portland Eastern Herald and Gazette of Maine*, 24 November 1796; for further details about the Portland season, see ads in this same paper from 21 November 1796 to 26 January 1797.

11. *Portland Eastern Herald and Gazette of Maine*, 24 November 1796.

12. Ibid., 28 November 1796.

13. Ibid., 1 December 1796.

14. Ibid., 22 December 1796.

15. Ibid., 12 December 1796.

16. Ibid., 16 December 1796.

17. Ibid., 26 January 1797.

18. For details of the second Portsmouth season, see the advertisements in the *Portsmouth New Hampshire Gazette*, 28 January, 1, 4, 15, and 25 February 1797.

19. McNamara, *American Playhouse*, p. 80 and Seilhamer, *History of the Theater* 3:254; the building is still standing and in use.

20. Charles Blake, *History of the Providence Stage* (Providence, R.I.: George H. Whitney, 1868), p. 82.

21. Seilhamer, *History of the Theatre* 3:262–63; McNamara, *American Playhouse*, p. 91; and Donald C. Mullin, "Early Theatres in Rhode Island," *The American Journal of Theatre History* 11 (November 1970): 184.

22. For details of the Newport season, see the ads appearing in the *Newport Mercury*, 28 March–11 April 1797.

23. For details of the Providence season, see ads appearing in the *Providence Gazette* and the *Providence United States Chronicle,* 20–27 April 1797.

24. *Providence United States Chronicle,* 27 April 1797.

25. *Newport Mercury,* 2 May 1797.

26. *Providence United States Chronicle,* 27 April 1797.

## Chapter 3. The John Street Theatre

1. See Sollee's letter to the *Charleston City Gazette and Daily Advertiser,* 1 March 1799.

2. William Dunlap, *Diary of William Dunlap* (New York: New York Historical Society, 1930), 1:137.

3. Ibid., pp. 127–28, and Eola Willis, *The Charleston Stage in the Eighteenth Century* (Columbia, S.C.: The State Company, 1924), p. 361.

4. *Hartford Courant,* 7 August 1797.

5. *Boston Federal Orrery,* 25 January 1796.

6. Bernard, *Retrospections,* p. 256.

7. Robert Burns, *Complete Works of Robert Burns* (Cambridge, Mass.: The Riverside Press, Houghton Mifflin, 1897), pp. 177–78.

8. Descriptions of the John Street Theatre appear in many of the histories. See especially McNamara, *American Playhouse,* pp. 54–55, 59–61, 62–66; see also Hugh F. Rankin, *The Theatre in Colonial America* (Chapel Hill: University of North Carolina Press, 1965), pp. 123–24.

9. For an especially good account, including details of casting and repertory, for Sollee's season at the John Street Theatre and the subsequent arrival of Wignell, see George Clinton Densmore Odell, *Annals of the New York Stage* (New York: Columbia University Press, 1927), 1:448–72. See also Dunlap, *Diary,* 1:138–66.

10. For details of the production history of *The Battle of Bunker Hill,* see Brander Matthews's introduction to the 1891 Dunlap Society edition of the play.

11. Burk's description of the battle scene is from his letter to John Hodgkinson quoted in Brander Matthews's introduction to the play. See. n. 10.

12. Dunlap, *Diary,* 1:144.

13. Ibid., p. 156.

14. John Daly Burk, *The Battle of Bunker Hill* (New York: The Dunlap Society, 1891), Introduction, p. 6.

15. Sollee's letter to the *Charleston City Gazette and Daily Advertiser,* 1 March 1799, includes an item of $60 for passage from New York to Charleston.

## Chapter 4. The Charleston Comedians

1. For descriptions of Charleston during this period, see George C. Rogers, Jr., *Charleston in the Age of the Pinckneys* (Norman: University of Oklahoma Press, 1969); Charles Fraser, *A Charleston Sketchbook, 1796–1806* (Charleston, S.C.: Carolina Art Association, 1940); Charles Fraser, *Reminiscences of Charleston* (Charleston, S.C.: John Russell, 1854); Alice R. Huger Smith and D. E. Huger Smith, *The Dwelling Houses of Charleston* (Philadelphia: J. B. Lippincott, 1917); and "Diary of Timothy Ford," *South Carolina Historical Magazine* 13 (July 1912).

2. For Charleston's theatrical history prior to 1797, see Willis, *The Charleston Stage,* pp. 3–337; see also James H. Dorman, Jr., *Theatre in the Ante-Bellum South* (Chapel Hill: University of North Carolina Press, 1967), p. 18; and Crawford, *Romance of the American Theatre,* p. 64.

3. For details of the Charleston season of 1797–98, including casting and repertory, see Willis, *The Charleston Stage*, pp. 341–412.

4. For an account of Sollee's dispute with Tubbs, Edgar, and the Whitlocks, see ibid., pp. 383–94.

5. Sollee's letter is printed in ibid., pp. 386–91; Tubb's letter in *Charleston S.C. State Gazette and Timothy's Daily Advertiser,* 1 March 1798; and Edgar's in *Charleston City Gazette and Daily Advertiser,* 5 March 1798.

6. *Hall's Wilmington Gazette,* 8 March 1798, announces a nine-night stand in Wilmington, N.C., beginning 9 March 1798. Tubbs, his wife, and Eliza are all billed in the only advertisement for the season.

7. For the Placide-Williamson-Jones engagement in Savannah, see J. Max Patrick, *Savannah Pioneer Theatre from Its Origins* (Athens: University of Georgia Press, 1953).

8. For details of the season of the Charleston Comedians, see *Charleston City Gazette and Daily Advertiser,* 9 April–2 May 1798.

## Chapter 5. A Legacy

1. For details of the Halifax, N.C., engagement, see *Halifax North Carolina Journal,* 23 July 1798.

2. Biographers of Poe have traditionally placed Mrs. Tubbs's death between Eliza's Charleston and Philadelphia engagements. In the light of the Halifax and Richmond appearances (see n. 1 and 7 for this chap.), of which Poe's biographers were evidently unaware, I have placed Mrs. Tubbs's death before Eliza's Richmond engagement. The Halifax ad announces the postponement of a performance owing to the "indisposition of Mrs. Tubbs." This would indicate that she was ill in Halifax. Had Mrs. Tubbs been alive, she would surely have been playing in Richmond.

3. There are many accounts of the yellow fever epidemic of 1798 in the histories, as well as many descriptions in the Philadelphia newspapers. For especially graphic details, see *Philadelphia Claypoole's American Daily Advertiser* from August through October 1798. For the extent of the epidemic, see William Currie, "Facts and Observations on the Origin and Nature of the Pestilential Yellow Fever" (Philadephia: Budd and Bartram, 1800).

4. The Fredericksburg engagement of the Virginia Company is recorded in the *Fredericksburg Virginia Herald* from 31 July to 15 October 1798.

5. There are no extant Petersburg papers for the period that the Virginia Company would have been in Petersburg; however, an advertisement in the *Federicksburg Genius of Liberty,* 13 November 1798, inquiring about the whereabouts of a lost trunk containing theatrical properties and costumes lost between "Osborn's and Petersburg" is signed "Anne West," the leading lady of the Virginia company. The letter is dated "Petersburg, October 22, 1798" and convinces me that the Virginia Company was in Petersburg during October 1798.

6. For a complete listing of this season, see Martin Shockley, *The Richmond Stage 1784–1811* (Charlottesville: University Press of Virginia, 1977), pp. 140–54.

7. For Eliza's Richmond debut, see *Richmond Examiner,* 13 December 1798. See also Suzanne Ketchum Sherman, "Post Revolutionary Theatre in Virginia, 1784–1810" (Masters thesis, College of William and Mary, 1950), p. 214.

## Chapter 6. The Chestnut Street Theatre

1. For details of the yellow fever epidemic, see sources cited for chap. 5. For statistics on deaths, see *Philadelphia Claypoole's American Daily Advertiser,* 22 September 1798. See also Van Wyck Brooks, *The World of Washington Irving* (Cleveland and New York: World Publishing Company, 1946), p. 25.

2. The relatively close proximity of the Philadelphia and Virginia companies made for a good deal of exchange and communication. William Green, co-manager of the Virginia Company, still played guest engagements in Philadelphia and often hired many of the actors from Wignell's company.

3. For biographical details on Thomas Wignell, see Bernard, *Retrospections*, pp. 32–33n, pp. 258–59; Dunlap, *Diary*, 1:177, 183; Arthur Hornblow, *A History of the Theatre in America* (Philadelphia and London: J. B. Lippincott, 1919), p. 171; Seilhamer, *History of the Theatre*, 3:177; William Burk Wood, *Personal Recollections of the Stage* (Philadelphia: Henry Cairy Bird, 1855), pp. 90–93; and Richardson Wright, *Revels in Jamaica* (New York and London: Benjamin Blom, 1969), p. 218.

4. For descriptions of the Chestnut Street Theatre, see McNamara, *American Playhouse*, pp. 104–16; Pollock, *Philadelphia Theatre*, p. 54; and Seilhamer, *History of the Theatre*, 3:145–48.

5. For the description of Philadelphia during this period, see William Priest, *Travels in the U.S.A.* (London: J. Johnson, 1802); William Birch, *The City of Philadelphia* (Philadelphia: Real Estate Trust Co., 1908): Duke D. LaRochefoucault Liancourt, *Travels through the U.S.A.* (London: R. Phillips, 1799), 2:321–89; Bernard, *Retrospections*, pp. 63–64.

6. Bernard, *Retrospections*, pp. 260–61.

7. From act 1, scene 1 of the play.

8. For details of the Philadelphia season of 1799, see Pollock, *Philadelphia Theater*, pp. 376–97. See also Charles Durang, *History of the Philadelphia Stage between the Years 1749 and 1855* (Philadelphia: University of Pennsylvania Library, 1868), pp 63–68.

9. Wood, *Personal Recollections*, p. 58.

10. See Quinn, *Poe*, p. 700, for Eliza's assignments during the Baltimore season of 1799.

11. For Tubbs's appearance at Eliza's benefit in Baltimore, see *Baltimore American and Commercial Advertiser*, 7 June 1799. This is the last record of a performance by him as an actor.

12. For details of the Philadelphia season of 1799–1800, see Charles Durang, *Philadelphia Stage*, pp. 63–68; Reese Davis James, *Old Drury of Philadelphia* (Philadelphia: University of Pennsylvania Press, 1933), pp. 1–2; and Pollock, *Philadelphia Theatre*, pp. 398–403.

13. For an especially thorough account of the history of ballad opera and comic opera, see Edmond McAdoo Gagey, *Ballad Opera* (New York: Columbia University Press, 1937).

14. Charles Durang, *Philadelphia Stage*, p. 64.

15. Ibid., p. 63; Wood, *Personal Recollections*, p. 67.

16. For especially vivid descriptions of Washington during this period, see Constance McLaughlin Green, *Washington, Village and Capitol 1800–1878* (Princeton: Princeton University Press, 1962).

17. I. A. Mudd, "Early Theatres in Washington City," *Records of the Columbia Historical Society* 5 (1902): 67, quoting *Washington National Intelligencer*, 26 November 1800.

18. For details of the first Washington season, see *Alexandria Times and District of Columbia Advertiser*, 22 August–6 September 1800; see also Mudd, "Early Theatres in Washington City," p. 65; Anna Maria Brodeau, "Thornton Diary," *Records of the Columbia Historical Society* 10:177–78; and Wood, *Personal Recollections*, pp. 55–57.

19. Eliza married Charles Hopkins immediately after joining him in Virginia (see next chap.). Since they were apart for the whole year preceding their marriage, I believe that they became engaged prior to Charles's leaving Philadelphia for Virginia.

20. For details of the Philadelphia season of 1800–1801, see James, *Old Drury*, pp. 4–5, and Charles Durang, *Philadelphia Stage*, pp. 68–70.

21. *Philadelphia Gazette of the U.S. and Daily Advertiser*, 5 August 1801.

22. For details of the history of the Southwark Theatre, see Pollock, *Philadelphia Theatre*, pp. 16, 17, 19, 20, 44, 57, and 65; for a description of the theatre, see McNamara, *American Playhouse*, pp. 52–55.

23. *Philadelphia Gazette of the U.S. and Daily Advertiser*, 5 August 1801.

24. *Philadelphia Aurora and Daily Advertiser*, 11 August 1801.

25. For details of casting and repertory for Eliza's first season at the Southwark, see Charles Durang, *Philadelphia Stage*, pp. 68–69; see also *Philadelphia Poulson's American Daily Advertiser*, 14 August–2 October 1801.

26. For details of the Philadelphia season of 1801–2, see Charles Durang, *Philadelphia Stage*, pp. 70–72, and James, *Old Drury*, pp. 5–6.

27. *The Portfolio* 2 (23 January 1801): 3.

28. Charles Durang, *Philadelphia Stage*, p. 70.

29. *The Portfolio* 1 (19 December 1801): 51.

30. Quinn, *Poe*, pp. 704–5.

## Chapter 7. "The Land of Hog, Hominey, and Hoe-Cake"

1. For details of casting, repertory, postponement of the opening, and the fever scare during the summer season of 1802 at the Southwark, see *Philadelphia Gazette of the United States* and *Philadelphia Poulson's American Daily Advertiser*, 5–19 July 1802.

2. No date has been established for Eliza's marriage to Charles Hopkins. She was first billed as Mrs. Hopkins in the *Alexandria Columbian Advertiser* on 11 August 1802. The last ad for the Southwark season appeared in *Philadelphia Poulson's American Daily Advertiser*, 17 July 1802, so that the marriage occurred between 17 July and 11 August 1802. See Quinn, *Poe*, p. 12.

3. For the information about Alexandria in 1802, see Frederick Gutheim, *The Potomac* (New York, Chicago, San Francisco: Holt, Rinehart & Winston, 1949), and Gay Montague Moore, *Seaport in Virginia* (Richmond: Garrett and Massie, Inc., 1949).

4. McNamara, *American Playhouse*, p. 103, and Sherman, ". . . Theatre in Virginia . . . ," p. 204. See also *Columbian Mirror and Alexandria Gazette*, 21 January and 9 March 1797, and *Alexandria Times and District of Columbia Daily Advertiser*, 17 May 1798.

5. Suzanne K. Sherman, "Thomas Wade West, Theatrical Impresario," *William and Mary Quarterly*, ser. 30, 9 (1952): 27–28.

6. *Alexandria Times and District of Columbia Daily Advertiser*, 6 July 1802.

7. For details of the Alexandria season of 1802, including the concert at Gadsby's Tavern, see ads in *Alexandria Advertiser and Commercial Intelligencer* and *Alexandria Columbian Advertiser*, 2 August–16 September 1802.

8. Deed records of the Historic Fredericksburg Foundation, Inc. indicate that the Fredericksburg Theatre was located on William and Prince Edward Streets. The opening performance was reviewed in the *Fredericksburg Virginia Herald* during September 1797 (letter to author from Ronald E. Shilby, Executive Director, Historic Fredericksburg Foundation, Inc., 11 January 1977).

9. John T. Goolrich, *Historic Fredericksburg* (Richmond: Whittel and Shepperson, 1922).

10. Dunlap, *Diary*, 2:387.

11. James G. Scott and Edward A. Wyatt IV, *Petersburg's Story, a History* (Petersburg, Va.: Titmus Optical Co., 1960), p. 40.

12. For especially good descriptions of life in Virginia at this time, see Bernard, *Retrospections*, pp. 146–75, and Benjamin H. LaTrobe, *The Journal of Benjamin H. LaTrobe* (New York: Burt Franklin, 1971).

13. For details of the Fredericksburg season of 1802, see ads in the *Fredericksburg Virginia Herald*, 17 September–12 October 1802.

### Chapter 8. "A Theatrical Fracas"

1. For information on the Back Street Theatre, see Edward Wyatt IV, "Three Petersburg Theatres," *William and Mary College Quarterly Historical Magazine*, ser. 2, 21 (April 1941).

2. For details in casting and repertory for the Petersburg season of 1802, see ads in the *Petersburg Intelligencer*, 16 November–10 December 1802. See also *Petersburg Republican and Advertiser*, 7 December 1802.

3. See Edward A. Wyatt IV, "John Daly Burk," *Southern Sketches*, no. 7, 1st ser. (Charlottesville, Va.: Historical Publishing Company, Inc., 1936).

4. *Petersburg Republican and Advertiser*, 7 December 1802.

5. For the description of the trip to Richmond as well as descriptions of the city itself, see Liancourt, *Travels*, 2:30–53, and Samuel Mordecai, *Richmond in By-Gone Days*, 2nd ed. (West and Johnston Publishing, 1860).

6. For details known of the Richmond season of 1802–03, see Shockley, *Richmond Stage*, pp. 163–71.

7. For a drawing of the Fenchurch Street Theatre, see *Norfolk Virginia Pilot*, 7 July 1940; see also George Holbert Tucker, "Early Norfolk Theatre," in the same issue of the *Norfolk Virginia Pilot* and McNamara, *American Playhouse*, pp. 89–102.

8. For descriptions of Norfolk during this period, see H. W. Burton, *The History of Norfolk Virginia* (Norfolk: Norfolk Virginian Job Print, 1957); Thomas J. Wertenbaker, *Norfolk, Historic Port* (Durham, N.C.: Duke University Press, 1931); and *Moreau de St. Mery's American Journey*, trans. and ed. Kenneth Roberts and Anna M. Roberts (Garden City, N.Y.: Doubleday and Company, Inc., 1947).

9. *Norfolk Herald*, 12 March 1803.

10. Ibid., 8 June, 23 November 1802, and 12 March 1803.

11. Ibid., 8 July 1800.

12. Ibid., 24 March 1803.

13. Two reviews of Eliza's first appearance in *The Highland Reel* appear in the *Norfolk Herald*, 14 April 1803. Both mention the fight.

14. For details of the 1803 spring season in Norfolk, see *Norfolk Herald*, 8 March–5 April 1803.

15. For details of the 1803 spring season in Petersburg, see *Petersburg Intelligencer*, 10–20 May 1803.

16. For details of the 1803 summer season in Norfolk, see *Norfolk Herald*, 4 June–12 July 1803.

### Chapter 9. David Poe

1. *Richmond Virginia Argus*, 23 July 1803.

2. For details of the Alexandria season of 1803, see *Alexandria Advertiser and Commercial Intelligencer*, 3 August–8 September 1803. See also *Alexandria Times and District of Columbia Daily Advertiser*, 22 August and 9 September 1803.

3. *Alexandria Times and District of Columbia Daily Advertiser*, 22 August 1803.

4. *Alexandria Advertiser and Commercial Intelligencer*, 6 September 1803.

5. An advertisement appears in the 8 October 1803 issue of the *Fredericksburg Apollo*. Both plays it announces were in the Virginia Company's repertory. No issues of the *Fredericksburg Virginia Herald* (the paper in which the Virginia Company usually advertised) are extant for this period. Since the company usually played in Fredericksburg this time of year, I assume that the advertisement in the *Apollo* indicates its usual season in Fredericksburg.

6. Two ads appear in the extant Petersburg papers from this period. One is the 1

November 1803 issue of the *Petersburg Intelligencer* and the other containing the ad for the Hopkinses' benefit.

7. *Petersburg Republican,* 11 November 1803.

8. For details of the Richmond season of 1803–4, see Shockley, *Richmond Stage,* pp. 171–86.

9. Wertenbaker, *Norfolk,* p. 142.

10. *Richmond Gazette and General Advertiser,* 17 March 1804.

11. For details of the 1804 spring season in Petersburg, see *Petersburg Intelligencer,* 17 April–22 June 1804.

12. *Petersburg Intelligencer,* 22 June 1804.

13. For details of the 1804 summer season in Richmond, see Shockley, *Richmond Stage,* pp. 190–202.

14. For the background on David Poe, see Quinn, *Poe,* pp. 13–20, 707–8; Mary E. Phillips, *Edgar Allan Poe the Man* (Chicago, Philadelphia, Toronto: John C. Winston Co., 1926), pp. 54–55; see also Eola Willis, "The Dramatic Career of Poe's Parents," *The Bookman* 64 (November 1926): 288–91.

## Chapter 10. Replacing Anne West

1. For details of the Fredericksburg season of 1804, see *Fredericksburg Virginia Herald,* 14 September–12 October 1804.

2. For details of the fall season of 1804 in Petersburg, see *Petersburg Intelligencer,* 16 October–27 November 1804.

3. *Petersburg Intelligencer,* 23 October 1804.

4. For a detailed account of Burr's visit to Petersburg, see Matthew L. Davis, *Memoirs of Aaron Burr* (New York: Da Capo Press, 1971), pp. 348–49.

5. For details of the Richmond season of 1804–5, see Shockley, *Richmond Stage,* pp. 204–14.

6. *Richmond Enquirer,* 3 January 1805.

7. Ibid., 25 January 1805.

8. From Anne West's obituary in *Richmond Enquirer,* 22 January 1805. Four other Virginia newspapers carried accounts of her death (letter to the author from James Meehan, Assistant Librarian, Virginia Historical Society, 25 May 1976).

9. For details of the Norfolk season of 1805, see *Norfolk Herald and Norfolk Gazette,* 18 March–2 July 1805.

10. For biographical information on Mrs. Wilmot, see Seilhamer, *History of the Theatre,* pp. 136–66 and Wood, *Personal Recollections,* pp. 60 62.

11. *Federal Gazette and Baltimore Advertiser,* 7 June 1805; *Baltimore American and Commercial Advertiser,* 7 June 1805.

12. *Richmond Virginia Gazette and General Advertiser,* 28 August 1805.

## Chapter 11. "An Affectionate Wife"

1. *Washington National Intelligencer,* 14 November 1805; see also Mudd, "Early Theatres in Washington City," pp. 71–72.

2. For a fellow actor's opinion of Hodgkinson's work, see Bernard, *Retrospections,* pp. 257–58.

3. From act 1, scene 2 of *Ways and Means.*

4. *Washington National Intelligencer,* 11 September 1805.

5. Hodgkinson's obituary appears in the *Washington National Intelligencer,* 16 September 1805.

6. For details of the Washington season of 1805, see *Washington National Intelligencer,* 9 September–9 October and 28 October–21 December 1805.

7. For details of the Fredericksburg season of 1805, see *Fredericksburg Virginia Herald,* 11–18 October 1805.

8. *Washington National Intelligencer,* 9 September 1805.

9. *Richmond Enquirer,* 5 November 1805.

10. *Washington National Intelligencer,* 27 November 1805.

11. For details of the Richmond season of 1806, see Shockley, *Richmond Stage,* pp. 215–31.

12. *Richmond Virginia Gazette and General Advertiser,* 15 January 1806.

13. For descriptions of the new Richmond Theatre, see *Richmond Deed Book,* 22, p. 289 (letter to the author from Mrs. Stuart B. Gibson, Librarian, Valentine Museum, 9 November 1972); see also Shockley, *Richmond Stage,* p. 215.

14. No definite date has been established for Eliza's marriage to David Poe. She was first billed as "Mrs. Poe" on 9 April 1806. For a discussion of this and a copy of the marriage bond, see Quinn, *Poe,* pp. 23–24.

## Chapter 12. "Her Best and Most Sympathetic Friends"

1. For details of the Warren and Wood season at the Chestnut Street Theatre during the summer of 1806, see *Philadelphia Poulson's American Daily Advertiser,* 17 June–8 July 1806.

2. *Philadelphia Poulson's American Daily Advertiser,* 18 June 1806.

3. For descriptions of Vauxhall Gardens and the theatre, see I. N. Phelps Stokes, *The Iconography of Manhattan Island,* (New York: R. H. Dodd, 1915–28), 5:1436, 1449, 1458, and 1461; see also Joseph N. Ireland, *Records of the New York Stage from 1750–1860* (New York: T. H. Morrell, 1866), 1:238 and Odell, *New York Stage,* 2:271.

4. *New York Evening Post,* 16 July 1806, carried an advertisement announcing Eliza's "debut."

5. *New York Morning Chronicle,* 17 July 1806.

6. *Boston Centinel,* 1 June 1796, carries an advertisement giving Mrs. Arnold's address on State Street.

7. For descriptions of Boston in 1806, see Harold and James Kirker, *Bullfinch's Boston* (New York: Oxford University Press, 1964), and Brett Howard, *Boston: A Social History* (New York: Hawthorn Books, Inc., 1976).

8. *The Polyanthos* 3 (September 1806): 141.

9. *Proceedings of the Massachusetts Historical Society* 59 (October 1925–June 1926): 322.

10. *The Polyanthos* 3 (October 1806): 206–7.

11. *The Emerald,* 25 October 1806.

12. *The Polyanthos* 5 (April 1807): 63.

13. *Boston New England Palladium,* 17 November 1806.

14. *Boston Columbian Centinel,* 14 January 1807.

15. For documentation of Henry's birth, see Quinn, *Poe,* pp. 16, 26.

16. *Boston Columbian Centinel,* 18 February 1806.

17. *The Emerald,* 21 February 1807.

18. For the version of *King Lear* current during Eliza's lifetime, see Elizabeth Inchbald, ed., *The British Theatre* (London: Longman, Hurst, Rees, and Orme, 1808), vol. 4, no. 1.

19. James Fennell, *Apology for the Life of James Fennell* (Philadelphia: Moses Thomas, 1814), pp. 373–74.

20. *The Polyanthos* 4 (March 1807): 281–82.

21. Ibid.

22. Joseph T. Buckingham, *Personal Memoirs and Recollections of Editorial Life* (Boston: Ticknor, Reed, and Fields, 1852), 1:57.

23. *Boston Columbian Centinel,* 25 February 1807.

24. Ibid., 18 March 1807.

25. *The Polyanthos* 4 (March 1807): 284.

26. *The Emerald,* 21 March 1807.

27. For details of the Boston season of 1806–7, see William W. Clapp, *A Record of the Boston Stage* (Boston: J. Monroe, 1853), pp. 88–89. For a listing of Eliza's and David's parts see Quinn, *Poe,* 712–16.

28. Maria Clemm's letter to Helen Whitman, dated 22 April 1859, printed in *Century Magazine* 77 (January 1909): 448–51.

29. Bernard, *Retrospections,* pp. 308–10.

30. *The Emerald,* 7 November 1807.

31. From the description of Rosamund in the play *Abaellino.*

32. *The Emerald,* 31 October 1807.

33. Ibid., 21 November 1807.

34. Ibid., 5 December 1807.

35. For Bernard's opinion of Mrs. Warren see Bernard, *Retrospections,* pp. 268–69.

36. See *Boston Gazette,* 12 December 1809; a souvenir edition of the text with a detailed description of the scenery and effects in this production is in the New York Public Library.

37. For a review of the performance, see *The Emerald,* 12 December 1807.

38. Most of Poe's biographers mention the sketch of Boston harbor. For the inscription, see Quinn, *Poe,* p. 35, quoting Mrs. Shew's letter to Ingram in the Ingram Collection, University of Virginia.

39. *The Emerald,* 9 January 1808.

40. Pierre Irving, *Life and Letters of Washington Irving* (New York: G. P. Putnam, 1862–64), 3:26.

41. *Boston Gazette,* 21 March 1808.

42. *The Emerald,* 16 April 1808; this issue also announces the Poe-Usher benefit.

43. See Bernard, *Retrospections,* pp. 291, 302, 312.

### Chapter 13. Roscius

1. *Petersburg Intelligencer,* 28 June 1808.

2. *Richmond Enquirer,* 8 July 1808; *Richmond Virginia Gazette and General Advertiser,* 8 July 1808.

3. *Petersburg Intelligencer,* 29 July 1808, and *Petersburg Republican and Advertiser,* 27 July 1808, both announce a performance for 2 August; *Petersburg Intelligencer,* 2 September 1808, announces a performance for 3 September.

4. For the repairs to the Federal Street Theatre during the summer of 1808, see Snelling Powell's letter to the trustees dated 15 June 1808 in the Allen A. Brown Collection in the Boston Public Library (MsTh 1 D 158).

5. Charles Durang, *Philadelphia Stage,* p. 76.

6. See Quinn, *Poe,* pp. 727–29, for a discussion of the location of Edgar's birthplace.

7. For George Poe's complete letter to William Clemm, Jr., see Quinn, *Poe,* pp. 31–33.

8. Ibid., pp. 32–33.

9. Payne's description of the Boston managers appears in a letter to his cousin Robert Treat Payne; see *John Howard Payne Letterbooks, 1809–1810* (Harvard Theatre Collection), p. 48.

10. For this quotation from Garrick about *Romeo and Juliet,* see the Advertisement, p.

A3, in Garrick's acting version, *Romeo and Juliet* by Shakespeare with an additional scene (London: Tonson & Draper, 1750).

11. *Boston New England Palladium*, 18 April 1809.

12. For details of the Boston season of 1808–9, see Clapp, *Boston Stage*, pp. 101–7; see also Bernard, *Retrospections*, pp. 336–40.

### Chapter 14. "A Mere Mark to Shoot At"

1. *Boston Gazette*, 15 May 1809.

2. Odell, *New York Stage*, 2:324.

3. See letter to Robert Treat Paine dated 11 June 1809, in *John Howard Payne Letterbooks 1809–1810*, p. 202.

4. *New York Commercial Advertiser*, 6 June 1809.

5. For details of the description of the Park Theatre, see McNamara, *American Playhouse*, pp. 132–42.

6. *New York Commercial Advertiser*, 8 September 1809.

7. *The Rambler's Magazine* (New York: D. Longworth, 1809–10), 2:26.

8. Bruce I. Granger and Martha Hartzog, eds., *The Complete Works of Washington Irving* (Boston: Twayne Publishers, 1977), pp. 12, 14.

9. *The Rambler's Magazine*, 1:18.

10. Ibid., p. 19.

11. Ibid., p. 21.

12. David Longworth is identified as the editor of *The Rambler's Magazine* in the October 1809 issue of the *New York Evening Post*; his description of his critic appears in *The Rambler's Magazine*, 1:110.

13. *The Rambler's Magazine*, 1:23.

14. *New York Evening Post*, 23 September 1809.

15. *The Rambler's Magazine*, 1:26.

16. Ibid., p. 27.

17. The verses appear in *The Rambler's Magazine*, 1:88. *Sur un POE de Chambre/ Rendons hommage au redacteur/Des Ramblers' Magazine/Il juge bien de chaque acteur/Les talens a la mine:/Suivant lui surtout/Jamais du bon gout/Monsieur Pho n'eut l'empreinte,/Son pere etait pot/Sa mere etait broc,/Sa grand mere etait pinte.* Translation: "On a Chamber Pot"/ Let us pay homage to the editor of *The Rambler's Magazine*/He can judge the talents of every actor by his face/Following him everywhere/Never in good taste/Mr. Pot/Poe bears the mark/His father was a pot/His mother was a pitcher/His grandmother was a pint.

18. *The Rambler's Magazine*, 1:92–93.

19. Ibid., p. 94.

20. Ibid., p. 96.

21. Ibid., p. 27.

22. *Something*, ed. by Nemo Nobody, Esq. (Boston: J. West, 1809–10), 1 (16 December 1809): 76.

23. *The Rambler's Magazine*, 1:100.

### Chapter 15. The Park Theatre

1. *The Rambler's Magazine*, 1:106.

2. *New York Evening Post*, 28 October 1809.

3. Ibid., 28 November 1809.

4. *The Rambler's Magazine*, 1:198.

5. Ibid., pp. 211–12.

6. *New York Evening Post*, 13 March 1810.

7. *William Dunlap, A History of the American Theatre* (New York: J. & J. Harper, 1832), 2:274–75.

8. For details of the Park Theatre season of 1809–10, see Odell, *New York Stage,* 2:326–42, and Ireland, *Records of the New York Stage,* 1:260–69.

9. *New York Columbian,* 28 June 1810.

10. Dunlap, *History,* 2:273.

11. For a description of the final scene in *The Caravan,* see Odell, *New York Stage,* 2:341.

12. *New York Columbian,* 2 July 1810.

13. Ibid.

### Chapter 16. "Oh! Sweet, Anna Page"

1. *Petersburg Intelligencer,* 6, 20, and 27 July 1810; *Petersburg Republican and Advertiser,* 23 and 30 July 1810.

2. Margaret West's obituary appears in the *Norfolk Gazette and Public Ledger,* 6 June 1810; two other Virginia newspapers noted her death, the *Richmond Visitor,* 16 June 1810, adding "relict of Mr. Thos. West, founder of the Virginia theatres."

3. For background on the Placides, see Hoole, *Ante-Bellum Charleston Theatre,* pp. 3, 218–19, and Willis, *Charleston Stage,* pp. 335–37.

4. For details of the Richmond seasons of 1810, see Shockley, *Richmond Stage,* pp. 305–28.

5. *Richmond Enquirer,* 21 September 1810.

6. The miniature of Eliza that appears as this book's frontispiece is now in the Free Library of Philadelphia. It was at one time in the possession of Edgar Poe, who gave it to Mrs. Marie Louise Shew, later Mrs. Houghton. Mrs. Houghton sent the miniature to Poe's biographer John Ingram. For many years thereafter its whereabouts were unknown, until 1955 when Ivan Kats, an American teaching French to American soldiers in Paris, discovered it in a Paris flea market. It then came into the collection of Col. Richard Gimbel, who presented it to the Free Library of Philadelphia. Letter to the author from Howell J. Heaney, Rare Book Librarian, Free Library of Philadelphia, 7 August 1974.

7. Ads for the Virginia Company's season in Fredericksburg appear in the 10 and 13 October 1810 issues of the *Fredericksburg Virginia Herald.* Eliza is not billed, but the company is the same with which she had been appearing in Petersburg and Richmond.

8. For details of the Norfolk season of 1810, see *Norfolk Gazette,* 28 November–21 December 1810.

9. For the documents relating to Rosalie's birth, see Quinn, *Poe,* p. 40.

10. Mrs. Clemm mentioned a nurse to Sarah Helen Whitman; see Mrs. Whitman's letter to Ingram dated 2 June 1874, listed as item #156 in John Carl Miller, *Ingram's Poe Collection* (Charlottesville: University of Virginia Press, 1960). See also Weiss, *Home Life of Poe,* pp. 1–4 and Quinn, *Poe,* pp. 730–31. The woman Mrs. Weiss mistakes as Eliza's mother was probably a nurse.

11. For details of the Charleston season of 1811, see Hoole, *Ante-Bellum Charleston Theatre,* pp. 77–78; see also ads in *Charleston Courier,* 7 January–20 May 1811, and *Charleston Times,* 2 April–20 May 1811.

12. *Charleston Courier,* 23 January 1811.

13. Hoole, *Ante-Bellum Charleston Theatre,* p. 4; for descriptions of the Charleston Theatre, see W. Stanley Hoole, "Two Famous Theatres of the Old South," *South Atlantic Quarterly* 36 (July 1937): 273–77; see also McNamara, *American Playhouse,* pp. 87–89.

14. *Charleston Courier,* 21 March 1811; *Charleston Times,* 16 April 1811.

15. For detailed announcements about Sully's benefit, see *Charleston Courier,* 11, 12, and 15 April 1811.

16. See chap. 7.
17. *Norfolk Herald,* 26 July 1811, the letter signed "Floretta."

## Chapter 17. "One of Its Chief Ornaments"

1. For details of the Norfolk season of 1811, see *Norfolk Herald* and *Norfolk Gazette,* 10 June–5 August 1811.
2. *Norfolk Herald,* 26 July 1811.
3. For details of the Richmond season of 1811, see Shockley, *Richmond Stage,* pp. 329–59.
4. *Richmond Enquirer,* 11 October 1811, advertises the "last night until Fredericksburg and Petersburg races," but there are no extant papers to tell if the Virginia Company gave performances in either Fredericksburg or Petersburg.
5. Hervey Allen, *Israfel* (New York: Farrar and Rinehart, Inc., 1934), p. 17, quoting Joshua L. Ellis's letter of 13 August 1811.
6. For a discussion of where Eliza was living in Richmond at the time of her death, see Quinn, *Poe,* pp. 45–46.
7. Ibid., p. 44, quoting the Mordecai MSS in the Duke University Library, Durham, N.C.
8. *Richmond Virginia Patriot,* 29 November 1811.
9. *Richmond Enquirer,* 29 November 1811.
10. Ibid., 10 December 1811; *New York Evening Post,* 16 December 1811; *Boston Patriot,* 18 December 1811; all have obituaries for Eliza.
11. *Richmond Virginia Patriot,* 10 December 1811.

## Epilogue. "Her Brief Career of Genius and of Beauty"

1. *Richmond Enquirer,* 28 December 1811, is filled with graphic details of the fire; see also the issues of 31 December 1811 and 2 January 1812.
2. For various accounts of the Richmond Theatre fire, see Shockley, *Richmond Stage,* pp. 360–82; see also *Richmond Enquirer,* 28, 31 December 1811 and 2 January 1812.
3. *Richmond Enquirer,* 31 December 1811.
4. Henry's poem is reprinted from *The North American* in Hervey Allen and Thomas Olive Mabbott, *Poe's Brother* (New York: George H. Doran and Company, 1926), p. 41.
5. Quinn, *Poe,* p. 89; Allan's letter to Henry hinting at Rosalie's illegitimacy is reprinted in most of Poe's biographies.
6. For documentation of John Allan's illegitimate children, see Quinn, *Poe,* pp. 168–69.
7. Allen and Mabbott, *Poe's Brother,* p. 34.
8. Sarah Helen Whitman's letter to John Ingram dated 2 June 1874, listed as item #156 in *John Ingram's Poe Collection.*
9. Mrs. Houghton's letter to John Ingram dated 16 May 1875, listed as item #226 in *John Ingram's Poe Collection.*
10. Frances Winwar, *The Haunted Palace* (New York: Harper, 1959), p. 22, quoting Thomas O. Mabbott.
11. For Edgar's beliefs as to his father's death, see his letter to Beverly Tucker dated 1 December 1835, quoted in Quinn, *Poe,* p. 237; see also Poe's letter to William Poe dated 20 August 1835 in *The Letters of Edgar Allan Poe,* ed. John Ward Ostrom (Cambridge: Harvard University Press, 1948), 1:66–69.
12. See Mrs. Clemm's letter to Sarah Helen Whitman, dated 22 April 1859, *Century Magazine* 77 (January 1909): 44–45.

13. For the spurious press clipping that for a while established David Poe's death in Norfolk, see Quinn, *Poe*, p. 44, n. 85.

14. J. H. Whitty, *The Complete Poems of Edgar Allan Poe* (Boston and New York: Houghton Mifflin, 1910), p. xxi, quoting Frederick W. Thomas, *Recollections of Edgar Allan Poe.*

15. For an account of the erection of the monument on Eliza's grave and its inscription, see Samuel Pendleton Cowardin, Jr., "A Mother of Genius," *Equity Magazine*, April 1928, p. 13.

# Bibliography

Alden, John. "A Season in Federal Street," *Proceedings of the American Antiquarian Society*, April 1955. Worcester, Mass.: American Antiquarian Society, 1955.

Allen, Hervey. *Israfel.* New York: Farrar and Reinhart, Inc., 1934.

———, and Thomas Olive Mabbott. *Poe's Brother.* New York: George H. Doran Co., 1926.

Armstrong, Margaret Neilson. *Fanny Kemble, a Passionate Victorian.* New York: Macmillan Co., 1938.

Bernard, John. *Retrospections of America, 1797–1811.* New York: Harper & Bros., 1887.

Birch, William (and Son). "Reproduction of Birch's celebrated historical views of Philadelphia published in the year 1800." Philadelphia: Real Estate Trust Co., 1908.

Blake, Charles. *An Historical Account of the Providence Stage.* Providence: George H. Whitney, 1868.

Bowen, Catherine Drinker. *Miracle in Philadelphia.* Boston and Toronto: Little Brown and Co., 1966.

Broadhurst, R. J. *A History of Pantomime.* New York: Citadel Press, 1901. Reprinted 1964 by Benjamin Blom.

Brooks, Van Wyck. *The World of Washington Irving.* Cleveland and New York: World Publishing Co., 1946.

Brown, T. Allston. *A History of the New York Stage.* New York: Dodd Mead and Co., 1903.

Buckingham, J. T. *Personal Memoirs and Recollections of Editorial Life.* Vol. 1. Boston: Ticknor, Reed & Fields, 1852.

Burk, John Daly. *The Battle of Bunker Hill.* Introduction by Brander Matthews. New York: The Dunlap Society, 1891.

Burns, Robert. *Complete Works of Robert Burns.* Cambridge, Mass.: Houghton Mifflin, 1897.

Burton, H. W. *The History of Norfolk, Virginia.* Norfolk: Norfolk Virginian Job Print Co., 1877.

Caldwell, John Edwards. *Tour Through Part of Virginia.* Richmond, Va.: The Dietz Press, Inc., 1951.

Carpenter, Stephen C. *The Mirror of Taste and Dramatic Censor.* Philadelphia: Bradford and Inskeep, 1810.

*Cinderella or the Little Glass Slipper.* As performed at the Boston Theatre. The scenery painted by Mr. Worrall and the pantomime got up by Sr. Cipriani. Published for the purchasers, 1807.

Clapp, William W. *A Record of the Boston Stage.* Boston: J. Munroe, 1853.

Coad, Oral S., and Edwin Mins, Jr. *The American Stage.* the Pageant of America Series, vol. 14. New Haven, Conn.: Yale University Press, 1929.

Cowardin, Samuel Pendleton, Jr. "A Mother of Genius," *Equity Magazine,* April 1928.

Crawford, Mary Caroline. *Romance of the American Theatre.* Boston: Little Brown and Co., 1913.

Currie, William. *Facts and Observations on the Origin and Nature of the Pestilential Yellow Fever.* Philadelphia: Budd & Bartram, 1800.

Davis, Matthew L. *Memoirs of Aaron Burr.* New York: Da Capo Press, 1971.

Doran, John. *Annals of the English Stage.* Vols. 1 and 2. New York: W. J. Widdleton, 1865.

Dorman, James H., Jr. *Theatre in the Ante Bellum South.* Chapel Hill: University of North Carolina Press, 1967.

Dunbar, Seymour. *A History of Travel in America.* New York: Tudor Publishing Co., 1937.

Dunlap, William. *The Diary of William Dunlap 1766–1839.* Vol. 1, November 1786–15 December 1798. New York: Printed for the N.Y. Historical Society, 1930.

———. *A History of the American Theatre.* New York: J. & J. Harper, 1832.

Durang, Charles. *A History of the Philadelphia Stage Between the Years 1749 and 1855.* Arranged and illustrated by Westcott. Philadelphia: University of Pennsylvania Library, 1868.

Durang, John. *The Memoir of John Durang.* Edited by Alan S. Downer. Pittsburgh: University of Pittsburgh Press, 1966.

*The Emerald.* Nos. 26, 43, 46, 47, 79, 80, 82, 84, 85, 89, and 103. Boston: Belcher & Armstrong, 1806–8.

*An Exact Description of the Two Fam'd Entertainments of Harlequin, Dr. Faustus, and the Necromancer, or Harlequin Dr. Faustus.* London: Printed for T. Payne, 1724.

Fennell, James. *An Apology for the Life of James Fennell.* Philadelphia: Moses Thomas, 1814.

Ffrench, Yvonne. *Mrs. Siddons.* London: Derek Verschoyle, 1936.

Ford, Paul Leicester. *Washington and the Theatre.* New York: The Dunlap Society, 1899.

Fraser, Charles. *A Charleston Sketch Book 1796–1806.* Charleston, S.C.: Carolina Art Association, 1940.

———. *Reminiscences of Charleston.* Charleston, S.C.: John Russell, 1854.

Gagey, Edmond McAdoo. *Ballad Opera.* New York: Columbia University Press, 1937.

Goolrich, John T. *Historic Fredericksburg.* Richmond, Va.: Whittel and Shepperson, 1922.

Granger, Bruce I., and Martha Hartzog, eds. *The Complete Works of Washington Irving.* Boston: Twayne Publishers, 1977.

Green, Constance McLaughlin. *Washington, Village and Capitol 1800–1878.* Princeton: Princeton University Press, 1962.

Gutheim, Frederick. *The Potomac.* New York, Chicago, and San Francisco: Holt, Rinehart & Winston, 1949.

Handlin, Oscar, ed. *This Was America.* Cambridge: Harvard University Press, 1949.

Harrison, Gabriel. *John Howard Payne, Dramatist, Poet, Actor, and Author of Home, Sweet Home! His Life and Writings.* Philadelphia: Lippincott and Company, 1885.

Harrison, James A., and Charlotte F. Dailey. "Poe and Mrs. Whitman." *Century Magazine* 77, no. 3 (January 1909): 448–51.

Hewitt, Bernard. *Theatre U.S.A.* New York: McGraw Hill, 1959.

Hoole, W. Stanley. *The Ante-Bellum Charleston Theatre.* Tuscaloosa: University of Alabama Press, 1946.

———. "Two Famous Theatres of the Old South." *The South Atlantic Quarterly* 36 (July 1937).

Hornblow, Arthur. *A History of the Theatre in America.* Philadelphia and London: J. B. Lippincott Co., 1919.

Howard, Brett. *Boston: A Social History.* New York: Hawthorne Books, Inc., 1976.

Hughes, Glenn. *A History of the American Theatre, 1700–1950.* New York: Samuel French, 1951.

Hutton, Lawrence, ed. *Opening Addresses Written for and Delivered at the First Performance in Many American Theatres.* New York: The Dunlap Society, 1887.

Ingram, John H. *Edgar Allan Poe, His Life, Letters, and Opinions.* London: John Hogg, 1880.

Ireland, Joseph N. *A Memoir of the Professional Life of Thomas Abthorpe Cooper.* New York: Dunlap Society, 1888.

———. *Records of the New York Stage from 1750–1860.* Vol. 1. New York: T. H. Morrell, 1866.

Irving, Pierre. *Life and Letters of Washington Irving.* New York: G. P. Putnam, 1862–64.

James, Henry. *The Scenic Art: Notes on Acting and the Drama 1872–1901.* Edited by Allan Wade. New York: Hill and Wang, 1957.

James Reese Davis. *Cradle of Culture.* Philadelphia: University of Pennsylvania Press, 1957.

———. *Old Drury of Philadelphia.* Philadelphia: University of Pennsylvania Press, 1932.

Kirker, Harold and James. *Bullfinch's Boston.* New York: Oxford University Press, 1964.

Lane, Wheaton J. *From Indian Trail to Iron Horse.* Princeton: Princeton University Press, 1939.

*Letterbooks of John Howard Payne.* In manuscript at the Theatre Collection, Harvard University.

LaTrobe, Benjamin. *The Journal of LaTrobe.* New York: Burt Franklin, 1971.

Liancourt, Duke D. LaRochefoucault. *Travels Through the United States of America.* London: R. Phillips, 1799.

McNamara, Brooks. *The American Playhouse in the Eighteenth Century.* Cambridge: Harvard University Press, 1969.

Melish, John. *Travels Through the United States in the Years 1806 and 1807, 1809, 1810, and 1811.* Philadelphia: Thomas and George Palmer, 1812.

Miller, John Carl. *Ingram's Poe Collection at the University of Virginia.* Charlottesville: University of Virginia Press, 1960.

Moore, Gay Montague. *Seaport in Virginia.* Richmond, Va.: Garrett and Massie, Inc., 1949.

Mordecai, Samuel. *Richmond in By-Gone Days.* Richmond, Va.: West and Johnston, 1856. Second edition, 1860.

*Moreau de St. Mery's American Journey 1793–1798.* Translated and edited by Kenneth Roberts and Anna M. Roberts. Garden City, N.Y.: Doubleday and Co., Inc., 1947.

Moreland, James. "The Theatre in Portland in the 18th Century." *New England Quarterly* 11 (June 1938).

Mudd, A. I. "Early Theatres in Washington City." *Records of the Columbia Historical Society* 5 (1902).

Mullin, Donald C. "Early Theatres in Rhode Island." *The American Journal of Theatre History* 11, no. 2 (November 1970).

Nicoll, Allardyce. *A History of English Drama 1660–1900.* Vols. 1–4. Cambridge: Cambridge University Press, 1952–59.

Odell, George Clinton Densmore. *Annals of the New York Stage.* Vols. 1 and 2. New York: Columbia University Press, 1927–49.

Paine, Robert Treat. *Works in Verse and Prose.* Boston: J. Belcher, 1812.

Patrick, John Max. *Savannah Pioneer Theatre from Its Origins to 1810.* Athens: University of Georgia Press, 1953.

Phillips, Mary E. *Edgar Allan Poe the Man.* Chicago, Philadelphia, Toronto: John C. Winston Co., 1926.

Poe, Edgar Allan. *The Complete Poems of Edgar Allan Poe.* Edited by J. H. Whitty. Boston and New York: Houghton Mifflin Co., 1911.

———. *The Letters of Edgar Allan Poe.* Vols. 1 and 2. Edited by John Ward Ostrom. Cambridge: Harvard University Press, 1948.

Pollock, Thomas Clark. *The Philadelphia Theatre in the 18th Century.* Philadelphia: University of Pennsylvania Press, 1933.

*The Polyanthos.* Vol. 3, August–November 1806; vol. 4, December 1806–March 1807; Vol. 5, April–July 1807. Boston: J. T. Buckingham.

*The Portfolio.* Vol. 1: no. 3 (17 January 1801); no. 51 (19 December 1801). Vol. 2: no. 8 (27 February 1802); no. 3 (23 January 1802); no. 12 (27 March 1802); no. 51 (17 April 1802).

Powell, Mary G. *The History of Old Alexandria, Virginia.* Richmond, Va.: The William Byrd Press, Inc., 1928.

Priest, William. *Travels in the United States of America.* London: J. Johnson, 1802.

*Proceedings of the Massachusetts Historical Society* 59 (October 1925–June 1926).

Quinn, Arthur Hobson. *Edgar Allan Poe.* New York and London: D. Appleton-Century Co., Inc., 1941.

———. *A History of the American Drama from the Beginning to the Civil War.* 2d ed. New York: Appleton-Century Crofts, Inc., 1951.

*The Rambler's Magazine and New York Theatrical Register.* Vols. 1 and 2. New York: D. Longworth, 1809–10.

Rankin, Hugh F. *The Theatre in Colonial America.* Chapel Hill: University of North Carolina Press, 1965.

Ritson, Anne. *A Poetical Picture of America.* London: Verner, Hood, and Sharpe, 1809.

Rogers, George C., Jr. *Charleston in the Age of the Pinckneys.* Norman: University of Oklahoma Press, 1969.

Scott, James G., and Edward A. Wyatt IV. *Petersburg's Story, a History.* Petersburg, Va.: Titmus Optical Co., 1960.

Seilhamer, George O. *A History of the Theatre.* vols. 1–3. Philadelphia: Budd and Bartram, 1800.

Shakespeare, William. *King Lear Altered as Performed.* New York: David Longworth, 1811.

Sherman, Susanne Ketchum. "Post Revolutionary Theatre in Virginia 1784–1810." Masters thesis, William and Mary College, Williamsburg, Va., 1950.

———. "Thomas Wade West, Theatrical Impresario." *William and Mary Quarterly* 9, 3d series (1952).

Shockley, Martin. *The Richmond Stage 1784–1811.* Charlottesville: University Press of Virginia, 1977.

Smith, Alice R., and D. E. Huger Smith. *The Dwelling Houses of Charleston, S.C.* Philadelphia: J. B. Lippincott Co., 1917.

Smith, William Loughton. Journal of William L. Smith, in *Proceedings of the Massachusetts Historical Society,* October 1917. Edited by Albert Matthews. Cambridge, Mass.: Cambridge University Press, 1917.

*Something.* Edited by Nemo Nobody Esquire. Vol. 1, no. 5 (16 December 1809). Boston: J. West, 1809.

Stein, Elizabeth. *David Garrick, Dramatist.* New York: Benjamin Blom, 1967.

Stokes, I. N. Phelps. *The Iconography of Manhattan Island.* Vol. 5, New York: R. H. Dodd, 1915–28.

*The Theatrical Censor and Critical Miscellany by Gregory Greyhorn, Esq.* Nos. 1–13, 27 September–30 December 1806.

Thornton, Mrs. William. "Diary of Mrs. William Thornton." *Records of the Columbia Historical Society* 10. Washington, D.C.: Columbia Historical Society, 1907.

Titus, Rev. Anson. Letter in *Tyler's Quarterly Magazine* 4 (April 1923).

Weiss, Susan Archer. *The Home Life of Poe.* New York: The Broadway Publishing Co., 1907.

Weld, Isaac. *Travels through the States of North America and the Provinces of Upper and Lower Canada during the Years 1795, 1796, and 1797.* London: J. Stockdale, 1799.

Wertenbaker, Thomas J. *Norfolk, Historic Port.* Durham, N.C.: Duke University Press, 1931.

Willis, Eola. *The Charleston Stage in the 18th Century.* Columbia, S.C.: The State Co., 1924.

———. "The Dramatic Career of Poe's Parents." *The Bookman* 64 (November 1926).

Winwar, Frances. *The Haunted Palace.* New York: Harper, 1959.

Wish, Harvey. *Society and Thought in Early America.* New York: London, Toronto: Longmans, Green and Co., 1950.

Wood, William Burk. *Personal Recollections of the Stage.* Philadelphia: Henry Cary Baird, 1855.

Woodberry, George E. *The Life of Edgar Allan Poe.* Vol. 1. New York: Biblo and Tannen, 1965.

Wright, Richardson. *Revels in Jamaica.* New York, London: Benjamin Blom, 1969.

Wyatt, Edward A. IV. "John Daly Burk." *Southern Sketches,* no. 7, 1st series. Charlottesville, Va.: Historical Publishing House, Inc., 1936.

———. "Three Petersburg Theatres." *William and Mary Quarterly Historical Magazine* 21, 2d series, no. 2 (April, 1941).

Young, William C. *Documents of the American Theatre.* Vol. 1. Chicago: American Library Association, 1973.

# Index